DEDICATION

To our pupils past and present
who have challenged us and shaped the way we think about ethics.

CONTENTS

1 BEGINNING OF LIFE

Who am I?
What constitutes life?
Is there an inherent value to life?
What rights am I afforded by warrant of being human?
Can I do anything to lose those rights?!

You will find that there are many differing answers to those questions, but understanding what it is to be an individual human being is key if we are to make informed ethical decisions, particularly in relation to Medical Ethics. Not surprisingly, it is an area filled with controversy and can be a particularly emotive debate. Genetics tells us that we share 98% of our genes with chimpanzees, and on a genetic basis, we can find a shared ancestry with a great number of organisms. So, what is it that gives people their moral and ethical superiority, and can it be justified?

The Beginning of Life

There is a huge difference of opinion as to what constitutes the beginning of life. The moment the sperm and egg fuse, a single cell zygote is formed, which is genetically unique. As a result, many believe that this constitutes the beginning of life, often signalling what it will potentially become. Others point to the moment of brain activity at around 8 weeks of development, whilst others argue it is viability – the point at which the foetus can exist independently from its mother. Others still argue that even this independent existence is not enough and that a being must possess certain characteristics such as recognition of the self – moving to a more philosophical rather than biological interpretation of 'life.' It is from this philosophical viewpoint that we begin to question when that life requires moral consideration.

Personhood

Your answer to questions such as 'what is a person?' will affect the way that you think about key issues arising from the beginning of life, the prolongation of life, all the way to life's end. When philosophers use the term 'personhood', they are conferring that being with the highest moral status, having the right to life and dignity.

For example, if you believe a foetus doesn't become a person until they are born, then the extraction of stem cells from a pre-embryo wouldn't bother you. But if you believe that embryo constitutes a small person, then the same act would be seen as monstrously cruel.

The UK Abortion Act was altered in 1990 because foetal viability had reduced to 24 weeks – implying that viability was considered enough to confer personhood and a right to life. However, this viability changes based on people's access to healthcare, and has continued to change as medical technology has advanced. Indeed, viability now sits at closes to 22 weeks, yet the UK government has voted against altering the law again.

At the other end of the scale, we also must ask what constitutes the death of a person. Does someone with no brain activity warrant protection - or is it acceptable to harvest them for their organs? Finally, we must also ask questions such as even if an individual is recognized as a person must their life be maintained at all costs - or is it ever right to end it prematurely?

Defining the limits of personhood have incredibly far-reaching consequences. Particularly in the field of medical ethics, it shapes our laws, the role of doctors, and even our values as a society.

DISCUSSION TASK: WHICH OF THE FOLLOWING POSSESS PERSONHOOD?

a. A six-month-old baby
b. Superman
c. A chimpanzee
d. A person on life support
e. A child with Edward's syndrome
f. A 39-week-old foetus
g. Serial killers
h. A dead person
i. An adult human

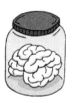

Can a brain in a jar have personhood?

ACADEMIC OPINION

John Noonan

John Noonan was a Roman Catholic philosopher and latterly, a law professor in America in the 1960s. Noonan was particularly interested in Roman Catholic moral doctrine and its relationship to law, which can be seen in his approach to personhood.

Noonan asserted that you could not argue with the fact that at conception, the new being receives its genetic code and that this signals it to be undeniable 'human'. It is this genetic information that determines its biology, key characteristics, and all the possibility of what they will become.

He recognised that genetic code is conceptually distinct from the concept of the 'moral person', given that genetic code is a matter of fact and moral person is a question of what value we then give. However, he asserted that genetic humanness is sufficient for moral personhood.[1]

What would you consider the pros and cons of his position?

Mary Anne Warren

Mary Anne Warren was a philosophy professor at San Francisco State University. Warren was particularly noted for her writings around the abortion debate and within animal rights. She has sometimes been described as a feminist, due to her pro-choice stance.

Warren focused on an individual's intellectual capacity or rather, cognitive function, to define personhood. According to her, personhood is present in those with the following traits:

1. *Consciousness (of things within and/or external to the self), and the capacity to feel pain.*
2. *Reasoning (the developed capacity to solve new and relatively complex problems).*
3. *Self-motivated activity (activity which is relatively independent of either genetic or direct external control).*

---

[1] John Noonan, *The Morality of Abortion: Legal and Historical Perspectives* (Harvard University Press, 1974).

4. *The capacity to communicate, by whatever means.*
5. *The presence of self-concepts, and self-awareness, either individual or racial, or both.*

Warren believed numbers 1 and 2 are probably necessary conditions for personhood and probably 1-3 are sufficient. However, she did not insist that any of these are absolutely necessary. However, she claimed that it is obvious that an individual that lacks all 5 is not a person.[2]

What would you consider the pros and cons of her position?

Social Criterion

Clifford Grobstein was as a leading American developmental biologist of the last half of the twentieth century. In his obituary in the New York Times, he was described as a 'Biologist Who Applied Ethics to Research'.

He asserted that from a biologist's perspective, personhood is certainly not achieved at conception. He cited examples such as monozygotic twinning, where two individuals are produced when one egg splits; he concluded that given this can happen at any point before 14 days then the pre-embryo can't possibly be deemed to be an individual person. He also highlighted the problem of anencephaly - where the foetus' brain fails to develop - claiming that in these instances that *'no true person [has been] produced at all'*[3]. As a result, he argued that it is beyond the ability of biology to determine the point at which personhood is established, and proposed that the key criterion is that personhood can be recognised by others. Those recognizing personhood at the moment of brain function, for example, are recognizing those signs as human and choosing to apply personhood to that individual.

What would you consider the pros and cons of his position?

Peter Singer

Peter Singer in an Australian moral philosopher, and a Professor of Bioethics at Princeton University. He is well-known as a Preference

---

[2] Mary Anne Warren, 'On the Moral and Legal Status of Abortion', *The Monist* 57/1 (1973).
[3] Clifford Grobstein, 'External Human Fertilisation', *Scientific American* 240 (1979).

Utilitarian.

Singer claims that to be 'persons' and to deserve moral consideration, beings must be self-aware, and capable of perceiving themselves as individuals through time. This criterion ignores the idea of species altogether and instead looks at a being's capacity to suffer. For Peter Singer, a person is a being who has a capacity for enjoyable experiences, for interacting with others and for having preferences about continued life. If a being cannot perceive suffering, or recognize that they are, then one need not factor them into moral consideration.

What would you consider the pros and cons of his position?

Gradient Theory

This theory, also known as gradualism, suggested that personhood is not binary but that it should be viewed on a scale of degrees. An embryo has less personhood than a foetus, a new-born would have more personhood than both, an infant more than an unborn foetus, a child more still, and so on. On the flipside, personhood can also be lost as gradually as it can be gained.[4]

What would you consider the pros and cons of this theory?

Having considered the relative merits of each of these theories, what is your overall judgement: which do you feel is the best solution and why?

---

[4] To read more about this theory, see Warren Quinn, 'Abortion, Identity and Loss', in *Bioethics*, ed. John Harris (Oxford University Press, 2001), 71.

2 SANCTITY OF LIFE

The sanctity of life, also known as the inviolability of life, is a fundamental concept that underpins many religious, philosophical, and ethical systems. At its core, it is a belief that certain aspects of life are so valuable and sacred that they should never be deliberately taken or destroyed. Proponents of the principle argue that all life is sacred and deserving of protection, regardless of circumstances or individual characteristics. However, its critics argue that it is overly simplistic and fails to consider the complexity of real-world dilemmas. For example, they might argue that in certain circumstances, such as self-defence or in war, taking a life may be necessary to protect other lives or prevent greater harm.

Religious views: Strong sanctity of life
The concept of the sanctity of life has its roots in many religious traditions, particularly in the context of Abrahamic religions such as Judaism, Christianity, and Islam. In these religions, the belief in the inherent value of human life is based on the idea that humans are created *'imago dei'*, or in the 'image of God'. This means that every human being has a divine spark that makes them unique and valuable. As a result of this belief, it is logical that human life should be protected and cherished.

St Thomas Aquinas was a medieval Italian theologian and philosopher who is widely regarded as one of the most influential thinkers in the Roman Catholic Church. He was born in 1225 in Italy, and entered the Dominican order at the age of 19. His most famous work is arguably his Summa Theologica, *a comprehensive study of theology and philosophy. Despite the work not actually being complete before his death, it remains one of the most significant and influential works in Western theology.*

In *Summa Theologica*, Aquinas discussed the sanctity of life and its implications for a wide range of ethical issues, including abortion, euthanasia, and suicide. For Aquinas, the sanctity of life extends to all stages of human existence, from conception to natural death. He maintained that we were not set up by God to allow self-destruction, and that as the author of life, only God has the right to determine its length. To destroy life is a violation of God's law and a rejection of His gift of life.[5]

Strengths

1. It is unequivocal. It is always wrong to kill another human being.
2. It promotes respect for human dignity. All human beings are made in the image of God: this equality can help to prevent

---

[5] For a full text of *Summa Theologica*, see https://sacred-texts.com/chr/aquinas/summa/, in particular question 64 ('of Murder').

abuses of human rights and ensure that all individuals are treated with kindness and compassion.

3. It encourages care for the vulnerable. Religious teaching on the sanctity of life often emphasizes the importance of caring for the poor, sick, and those with disabilities. It can inspire societies to work towards social justice and ensure services are provided for those in need.

4. By rejecting practices such as abortion, euthanasia, and assisted suicide, proponents must then work towards alternatives that prioritize life and human dignity.

Weaknesses

1. There is lack of consensus within religions. Even within a single religious tradition there may be disagreement on what constitutes the sanctity of life and how to apply it in practice. For example, Orthodox Jews would argue that every effort should be made to preserve life, whereas Reform Jews would allow for the withdrawal of medical help to allow death to happen.

2. It can be seen as inflexible. If a woman will die as a consequence of pregnancy, is it still wrong to destroy the foetus?

3. A gift we cannot reject is not a gift. If life is a 'gift' then ownership should pass to the recipient and the giver should have no further claim on the gift.

4. It can be seen as anthropocentric. The sanctity of life principle prioritizes human life over other life forms which can lead to neglect or exploitation of the environment and non-human species.

Deontological views

Beyond religious traditions, the sanctity of life is also the core principle in many philosophical and ethical systems as well. For example, in deontological ethical systems, such as Kantian ethics, the value of human life is considered absolute and non-negotiable.

Immanuel Kant was an eighteenth-century German philosopher who is known for his work on ethics, metaphysics, epistemology, and aesthetics. Whilst Kant did not explicitly use the term 'sanctity of life', his ethical theory is often cited as a basis for understanding the importance of human life.

Kant's view on the sanctity of life is based on his concept of the 'categorical imperative,' which is a moral principle that applies universally to all rational beings. The categorical imperative states that one should always act in such a way that the principle of one's actions could become a universal law. In other words, Kant believes that we should only act in ways that we would want everyone else to act in similar situations.

Kant believed in the inherent worth and dignity of every person, which he referred to as the 'dignity of humanity.' He argued that human beings have a unique moral status because they possess rationality and autonomy, and that they should be treated as an end in themselves rather than means to an end. Human beings have a moral duty to respect the dignity of others, which includes a duty to preserve and protect their lives.

Applied to the issue of the sanctity of life, Kant's view implies that human life must be treated as valuable and inviolable because it is a necessary condition for the moral agency of rational beings. To take a life, according to Kant, is to undermine the moral values that make human life worth living.

Strengths

1. It provides clear moral guidelines. The categorical imperative provides an objective criterion for assessing the morality of actions and a practical way to solve complex moral issues.
2. It gives the individual absolute protection from others and clearly affirms that the fundamental right for all humanity is the right to live. There is no personal preference or cultural bias. It places an obligation on society to see life as its priority and to ensure that this right is inviolable.
3. It affirms the responsibility that every individual must maintain and sustain their life regardless of circumstances, thus promoting stability in society where individuals are expected to meet their obligations.

Weaknesses

1. It is inflexible. Kant's theory applies to all rational beings, which can limit its use in certain situations. For example, the principle of the sanctity of life may conflict with other moral principles, such as the right to autonomy or the duty to alleviate suffering.
2. There is a lack of guidance on how to balance conflicting duties or interests.
3. Only rational beings have inherent value and dignity. This could lead to a hierarchy of human life where those who are not capable of rational thought or decision-making, such as infants or individuals with cognitive disabilities, are considered to have less worth.

Weak sanctity of life

Most ethicists think that human life is in some sense sacred, that humans have a special dignity that goes beyond that of other animals, and that there is something inherent about us that means we are valuable. It is hard to construct an ethical system without placing some sort of value on humanity. In this sense, 'sanctity of life' could be seen as a very broad concept. As we have seen, for most monotheists in the Judeo-Christian-Islamic tradition, this is connected to being made in the image of God. For many other ethicists, it is simply the sense that we have a common humanity.

However, we can see that the strong sanctity of life views held by the Roman Catholic Church, many evangelicals, and others, are quite extreme in the way they always put the sanctity of life before other ethical concerns such as comfort, autonomy and practicality. They also define it narrowly as protecting or preserving life, for example in the cases of abortion and assisted dying. Many ethicists prefer 'weak' sanctity of life views, in which they acknowledge the significance of the sanctity of life but say other ethical concerns also matter. An example of this is situation ethics.

Situation ethics
Joseph Fletcher was an American Christian philosopher and Episcopal priest, and he developed the philosophy of Situation Ethics in the 1960s. This rejected many traditional rule-based religious ethical systems, including rigid 'strong' sanctity of life doctrines, and argued that a truly Christian ethical system only needs to be based on one principle: agape or self-giving love. This was a consequentialist ethical system, meaning in any situation you could ask 'what is the most loving thing to do?' and change your actions to suit what you think the consequence will be. Fletcher justified this by referring to Jesus' radical teachings, criticism of the strict moral teachings of the Pharisees of his day, and self-giving love.

This has radical implications as a religious approach to Medical Ethics and the Sanctity of Life, as it means that traditional moral statements such as 'do not kill' are less important that 'love your neighbour'. Therefore, if killing someone is the most loving thing to do, according to Fletcher, it becomes a moral act. This point of view has been very influential on Liberal Christians, many Reformed Jews, and others, for whom it offers a more progressive social stance within a religious framework. More traditional theists have criticised Fletcher for 'selling out' and abandoning traditional morality, and he is reputed to have abandoned his Christian belief later in life.[6]

Strengths

1. People are free to make their own moral choices and have a comprehensive guiding principle to follow.
2. Flexibility and finding a moral middle ground is seen as positive.

Weaknesses

1. By placing so much emphasis on individual choice in ethics, it allows for a very subjective interpretation of ethics in which problematic actions such as non-voluntary euthanasia could be justified by the idea that they are 'loving'.
2. It doesn't actually tell people what is right and wrong.

Utilitarian views

Peter Singer and other Utilitarians reject traditional Sanctity of Life views completely, describing it as a 'misplaced doctrine' that prevents us from making sensible decisions. He also states that 'the biological facts upon which the boundary of our species is drawn do not have moral significance'.[7] This means that just because something or someone can be seen to be human does not mean that they are sacred or have a particular moral value.

Libertarian views

The fundamental question at the heart of the puzzle is related to the source or origin of the sanctity of life. The deontological perspective posits that the intrinsic value of life is what confers sanctity, whereas

---

[6] Joseph Fletcher's views on Medical Ethics are most clearly shown in his book *Humanhood* (Prometheus, 1979).
[7] Peter Singer, *Rethinking Life and Death* (Oxford University Press, 1994), 97.

the Christian perspective suggests that sanctity is a result of divine decree. However, the third viewpoint, that of the Libertarian, considers human autonomy key – the ability for humans to make their own decisions without reference to anyone. According to this view, individuals hold the right to make decisions about their own bodies and dispose of them as they see fit. The sanctity of life is still upheld for others, as everyone has the right to not be killed by others. The only individual who can take away their own life is themselves. As a result, Libertarians would be against any law that they view as restrictive or limiting to individual freedom and autonomy.

Strengths

1. There is an emphasis on personal responsibility. Individuals should take responsibility for their own choices and actions, rather than relying on others to solve their problems.
2. Individuals should not be forced. Libertarians would wish to avoid situations in which the vulnerable felt they were coerced in any way e.g. choosing to die because they feel as if they are wasting resources.

Weaknesses

1. Humans are not autonomous beings in the strict sense of the word. Humans are social beings and the actions of one human being will inevitably impact society as whole. There is a lack of concern for the collective well-being.
2. There is a lack of guidance on how to balance the needs of the many against the individual. Whilst libertarians generally support limited government interference, they can sometimes overlook the role that government can play in promoting the common good, protecting the environment, and ensuring social justice.

TASK

	Religious	Non-religious
Rule-based	Roman Catholic Church/Evangelicals	Deontology (Kant)
Consequentialist	Situation Ethics (Joseph Fletcher)	Utilitarianism Libertarianism

Shading indicates stronger Sanctity of Life views.

Where would you place your own views on this table? Which views are closest to your own?

DISCUSSION TASK: TOM'S DECISION

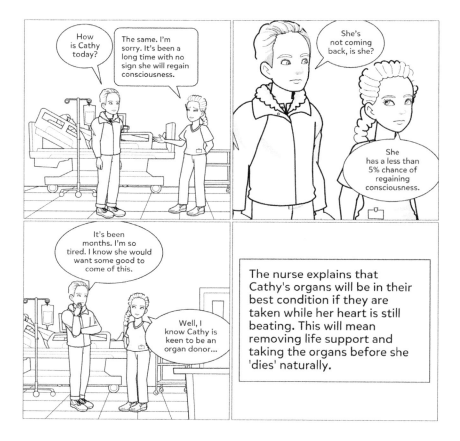

If Tom decides to opt for Cathy's organs to be donated, they could save up to nine lives. He has the following choices:

a) He can keep Cathy on life support in the hope that she will eventually regain consciousness. This will put pressure on the health service and will be costly in terms of resources.

b) He can ask for Cathy's life support to be removed so she can die naturally if her brain is already unresponsive.

c) He can opt for Cathy's organs to be harvested while she is still on life support, meaning that her heart will still be providing her organs with vital blood until just before they are removed. This allows for the strongest chance that organ transplants to others will be successful.

In this situation, what would each of the following do and why?

a) A believer in the strong sanctity of life, such as a Roman Catholic.
b) A Deontologist.
c) A Situation Ethicist.
d) A Utilitarian.
e) You!

3 TREATMENT AND USE OF EMBRYOS

The treatment and use of embryos refers to the methods and techniques used in medical research and clinical practice that involve the manipulation and experimentation on human embryos. This can include in-vitro fertilization (IVF) and embryo transfer, as well as research involving the genetic modification of embryos for therapeutic purposes. The ethical questions surround the treatment and use of embryos often centre around the moral status of the embryo and whether it is considered a human life deserving of protection and respect.

There is no doubt that pregnancy and childbirth carry many potential difficulties and risks. For instance, it is estimated that 1 in 6 couples across the world encounter difficulties with fertility.[8] Additionally, in women under 30, one in 10 pregnancies may end in miscarriage, with this rate increasing as age advances, reaching more than five in 10 pregnancies in women over 45. Every year, approximately 30,000 babies and children get newly diagnosed with genetic conditions, and over 2.4 million children and adults are living with these ailments in the UK. According to research conducted by the University of Oxford in 2022,

---

[8] See this article from April 2023 for more detail:
https://www.who.int/news/item/04-04-2023-1-in-6-people-globally-affected-by-infertility

maternal mortality rates in the UK have increased, with 9.6 Maternal deaths for every 100,000 babies born. Among all European countries, the UK has the second highest maternal death rate.

Now, envision a future in which these risks are eliminated: You're on your way to work, riding on a hover train powered by potato skins, munching on a sandwich filled with fat-reducing bacon. The two people seated opposite you are exchanging stories about clones, whilst a nearby couple is debating which box to check - should they pay extra for musical or sporting ability? You pull up the news on your tablet and read, 'Retirement age to rise to 105'.

Whilst this may seem like a dystopian future, research to bring about these possibilities has been progressing since 1878. It was then that basic research into gametes began, which eventually led to the world's first 'test tube baby' – Louise Brown – being born in England in 1978. Eggs were harvested from her mother, inseminated using her father's sperm in the lab, before being transplanted back into her mother's womb. Today over 10 million children have been born as a result of this technology. 2% of children born in the UK are now conceived using In Vitro Fertilization (IVF).

Whilst it can be used to help people who struggle with infertility, it can also help people with a serious inherited disease in their family. IVF can involve the use of the couple's own eggs and sperm, or it may involve the use of donor eggs, donor sperm, or both. The embryos can be tested (or screened) so that only healthy embryos are placed into the womb.

Mitochondrial donation treatment can also be used by people who are at risk of passing on a serious mitochondrial disease to any children they might have. The treatment involves transferring the nuclear genetic material from the mother's eggs or embryos into a donor egg or embryo with healthy mitochondria. Any children would still be the mother's and father's biologically – because the genetic material is found in the nucleus – but without the mitochondria that cause the disease.

The IVF process typically involves several steps, including:

1. Ovarian stimulation: the woman is given fertility drugs to stimulate her ovaries to produce multiple eggs.
2. Egg retrieval: the eggs are harvested from the woman's ovaries using a needle guided by ultrasound.
3. Sperm collection: the man provides a semen sample, which is then prepared in the lab to isolate the healthiest and most active sperm.
4. Fertilization: the eggs are mixed with sperm in a laboratory dish for fertilization.
5. Embryo culture: the fertilized eggs are monitored and cultured for several days to allow them to develop into embryos.
6. Embryo transfer: one of more embryos are transferred into the woman's uterus using a thin catheter.
7. Pregnancy test: the woman takes a pregnancy test about two weeks after the embryo transfer to determine if the IVF cycle was successful.

Throughout the IVF process, the woman will undergo regular ultrasounds and blood tests to monitor hormone levels and the development of her eggs. The process typically takes several weeks to complete. The embryos that are 'left over' from this process, with the consent of the parents, may then be used for research purposes.

The HFEA

The HFEA (Human Fertilisation and Embryology Authority) is a UK government regulatory body that oversees and regulates human embryo research, as well as fertility treatments and donation of eggs, sperm and embryos. The HFEA was established in 1990 under the Human Fertilisation and Embryology Act, and since then has been responsible for licensing and monitoring fertility clinics and research labs in the UK.

In 1982, British Philosopher Mary Warnock was challenged with running the Human Fertilisation and Embryology Committee and drafting new regulations. They founded the HFEA and created the 1990 Human Fertilisation and Embryology Act.

It is legal to use human embryos for research purposes, subject to strict regulations and ethical guidelines. Embryos are not allowed to be used for more than 14 days after fertilization and can only be utilized for research that seeks to:

- Expand understanding and discover treatments for severe illnesses.
- Develop novel fertility treatments.
- Gain knowledge of miscarriages.
- Improve methods of contraception.
- Create approaches for assessing embryos for genetic diseases before implantation.
- Advance knowledge of embryo development.

The so-called '14 day rule' is based on the moment of 'gastrulation', when embryonic cells begin to specialise. Before this time, all embryo cells are the same, 'stem cells', with the ability to become different types of cell. After gastrulation, different features begin to develop within the embryo, eventually leading to the central nervous system and heartbeat. Warnock and her colleagues reasoned that there was no possibility of an embryo feeling pain or being aware before 14 days as it does not have any nerves or ability to experience. The significance of regulation lies in its ability to guarantee that work must be carried out to specific standards, that only qualified individuals are authorized to perform it, and that research on embryos is undertaken solely when it is necessary and in an ethical manner.

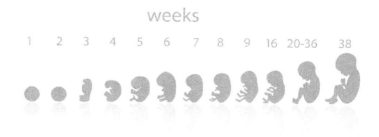

In 2008, the Human Fertilisation and Embryology Act was updated to allow for several new technologies, including:

- Saviour siblings (see below)
- 'Three-person babies' (to treat mitochondrial disease, see above)
- Chimeras, with a mixture of human and animal DNA (these can only be kept for up to 14 days and are for research purposes such as genetic testing for animal organ transplantation)

Any embryos that are not implanted into a uterus must still be disposed of by 14 days.

MORAL ISSUES

The ethical dilemma of designer babies

CRISPR technology, which stands for Clustered Regularly Interspaced Short Palindromic Repeats, is a revolutionary gene-editing tool that enables scientists to manipulate genetic material with unprecedented precision. The technology has been described as a 'molecular scalpel' and has the potential to cure genetic disease, enhance human performance, and even create 'designer babies.' Designer babies are children whose genetic makeup has been altered to enhance their physical or intellectual traits, and CRISPR technology has made this controversial idea a tangible possibility. However, the ethical implications of such a practice have sparked a heated debate among scientists and philosophers alike.

On the one hand, proponents of designer babies argue the technology could be used to eliminate debilitating genetic diseases such as cystic fibrosis, sickle cell anaemia, and Huntington's disease. By editing the genes responsible for these conditions, scientists could prevent them from being passed down to future generations. Additionally, CRISPR technology could be used to enhance desirable traits such as intelligence, athleticism, and height, which could have significant benefits for society as a whole.

On the other hand, critics of designer babies argue that the technology raises a host of ethical concerns. They worry it could lead to a new form of eugenics, in which children are genetically engineered to meet certain societal standards. They also worry that it could exacerbate existing inequalities by creating a new class of genetically superior individuals who have access to the technology. Moreover, they argue that the long-term effects of gene editing are largely unknown, and that they could be unintended consequences that we cannot predict.

To Discuss

Which of the following would you deem acceptable?

- The correction of the chromosomal abnormality which causes Down's syndrome.
- The manipulation of the chromosomes which determine the sex of a person.
- The manipulation of the genes which determine a person's height.
- The correction of the genetic causes of Huntingdon's disease.
- The manipulation of the genes to ensure deafness.
- The manipulation of the genes which determine a person's skin colour.

What is the moral status of the embryo?
Some people believe that embryos have the same moral status as fully developed human beings, and therefore, it is wrong to use them for research or destroy them. They argue that embryos are potential persons with the right to life and that it is unethical to treat them as mere objects or raw materials for scientific experimentation.

Others argue that embryos have a lesser moral status than fully developed human beings because they lack consciousness, self-awareness, and other attributes that are typically associated with personhood. They contend that embryos are not yet persons and that their use for research can benefit society by advancing medical knowledge and developing new therapies. Whilst sperm, eggs, and pre-embryos all have the potential to become persons, they equally have the potential to become no persons at all. It is only after 14 days when the cells have developed into one or more individuals, therefore it is contended that it is only after that point that it should be given a moral status.

To what extent should informed consent be sought?

Consent is an issue in relation to embryo research because embryos are typically created for reproductive purposes, and their use for research involves a significant departure from the original intent of their creation. Therefore, obtaining informed consent from the individuals who donate embryos or the couples who undergo fertility treatments is essential – and required by UK law – to ensure that their rights and interests are respected.

Informed consent means that individuals are fully informed about the nature, purpose, risks, and benefits of the research, and they voluntarily agree to participate based on their understanding and free will. However, obtaining informed consent for embryo research can be challenging for several reasons.

First, embryos are often created from the eggs and sperm of multiple donors, which can complicate the consent process, as it may be difficult to identify and contact all the parties involved. Second, the donors may have different views on the use of their embryos for research. Third, the long-term implications of embryo research are uncertain, and the donors may not fully understand the potential risks and benefits of the research.

It almost goes without saying that the embryo itself cannot give informed consent. Thus, questions about the protection of vulnerable populations and the potential for commercial exploitation are raised.

Should all people have access to fertility treatment?

For many, fertility treatment is a fundamental human right. The Universal Declaration of Human Rights states that *'everyone has the right to a standard of living adequate for the health and well-being of himself and his family, including good, clothing, housing, and medical care.'* Infertility is a medical condition that can cause emotional distress and psychological suffering for couples who want to conceive. It follows that to deny access to fertility treatment would be a violation of their human rights.

In Scotland the NHS offers IVF treatment to couples who meet certain criteria: the woman must be between 18 and 40 years old, the couple must have been trying to conceive for at least two years, or have a diagnosed fertility problem, both partners must be non-smokers, the couple must have a Body Mass Index (BMI) of less than 30, and the woman must have a good chance of carrying the pregnancy to term. In addition to this, the couple must have no living children from their current relationship, and they must be in a stable and supportive relationship. In 2008, Scotland became the first part of the UK to provide IVF treatment to same-sex couples, with the same criteria applying to same-sex and oppositive-sex couples.

However, the question arises whether the Government, by denying treatment to couples who do not meet the criteria, is in fact, violating human rights?

On the flip side, one could question whether the right to medical care really extends to fertility. The ultimate aim of fertility treatment is to generate a new life – to what extent should we have the right to acquire another human being?

Is IVF or embryo selection 'playing God'?

The idea of 'playing God' is a common argument against genetic engineering. It suggests that by interfering in the reproductive process, or by manipulating the genetic makeup of living organisms, humans are taking on the role of a creator. However, this argument is subjective and depends on one's beliefs about the nature of God and the role of humans in the universe. For example, could it be that God endowed us with the intelligence and ability to discover genetic engineering, and created us with a moral compass to lead us to its uses? By being created in his image, does it not follow that we are able to share his creative ability?

This in turn, leads to further issues: who is to say whose moral compass is correct? Some of those representing people with disability believe that if you are trying to eliminate known health problems, this implies that people with those problems are less worthy of respect that other people. To say that they would be better off if they had been engineered to be 'healthy' is seen as insulting. But some rights advocates would take things even further and argue that the technology could be used to select a consisting that is usually regarded as a disability. For example, if two deaf parents wanted a deaf child to be able to be more included in their community. Who is to say this is wrong?[9]

Are 'saviour siblings' ethical?
Saviour siblings are children who are conceived through IVF and genetically selected to be a bone marrow or organ donor for a sibling with a life-threatening illness. This process involves screening embryos for a genetic match to the sick sibling before implanting the selected embryo in the mother's uterus.

The ethical implications of saviour siblings are complex. Supporters argue that saviour siblings offer a chance for sick children to receive life-saving treatment from a genetically matched donor and can help families avoid the emotional and financial burden of finding a compatible donor. They also argue that parents have the right to use reproductive technology to give their children the best chance of

---

[9] See Jacqueline Mae Wallis, 'Is it ever permissible to select for deafness in one's child?' *Medicine, Health Care and Philosophy* 23 (2020), 3-15.

survival.

Critics, on the other hand, argue that saviour siblings are a form of commodification of children, where children are created to serve the needs of others. They argue that the process is morally problematic because it involves creating a child for a specific purpose rather than for the sake of the child itself. Critics also raise concerns about the potential physical and emotional risks to the saviour sibling, as the procedure involves invasive medical procedures and the potential for psychological harm. Likewise, the saviour sibling has no choice or autonomy as to whether they will participate in the procedure.

From a deontological perspective, an action is right or wrong based on whether it adheres to a set of moral rules or duties. For example, Immanuel Kant argued that we must always act out of respect for the moral law, which is based on reason and applies to all rational beings. In the case of saviour siblings, deontology would examine the duties and principles involved. For example, deontologists may argue that parents have a duty to provide the best possible care for their existing child, and that creating a saviour sibling is a morally justifiable way of fulfilling that duty. But conversely, they may also argue that creating a saviour sibling involves treating the child as a means to an end, rather than as an end in themselves. This would be a violation of the moral principle of respect for persons. This presents a conflicting imperative, the outcome of which is entirely dependent on how one weighs the various moral principles involved.

RELIGIOUS RESPONSES

The Roman Catholic Church
The Roman Catholic Church is the largest Christian denomination in the world, with over 1.3 billion members worldwide. It is headed by the Pope who is considered the spiritual leader of the Catholic Church. The Vatican is the headquarters of the Catholic church and is the residence of the Pope but is also home to many important Catholic institutions. The Vatican is a sovereign state, which means that it has its own

government, laws, and currency. The Catholic Church traces its origins back to Jesus' disciples and is generally considered to be a conservative form of Christianity.

The Catholic Church does not support in vitro fertilization (IVF) as it involves the manipulation and destruction of embryos, which the Church considers to be human beings which therefore have the right to life. The Congregation for the Doctrine of Faith, a Vatican department responsible for promotion Catholic doctrine, issued a document in 1987 called *Donum Vitae*, which outlined the Church's position on reproductive technologies, including IVF.[10]

The document recognises the scientific advancements in embryology and acknowledges the importance of studying the development of human life. However, *Donum Vitae* emphasises the intrinsic value and dignity of human life from the moment of conception. It states that every human being has the right to life and that this right should be protected from conception to natural death. The document condemns any form of experimentation, manipulation, or destruction of human embryos. Furthermore, *Donum Vitae* discusses the moral implications of IVF and other assisted reproductive technologies. It recognizes the possibility of these technologies helping infertile couples conceive, but it also highlights the risks and ethical concerns associated with them. Given that IVF can involve the creation of multiple embryos, questions about the fate of the 'unused' embryos are raised. *Donum Vitae* also discourages the freezing and storage of embryos arguing that it 'constitutes an offence against the respect due to human beings by exposing them to grave risks of death or harm.'

Instead, the Roman Catholic Church argues that people must recognise that God made us the way we are. If we are infertile, that could be a gift from God and should be treated as such. Perhaps God is freeing us to do

---

[10] For a full text of *Donum Vitae*, see
https://www.vatican.va/roman_curia/congregations/cfaith/documents/rc_con_cfaith_doc_19870222_respect-for-human-life_en.html

some other works for him, such as to help foster or adopt children. To tamper with the way God made things is 'playing God' and is not a good thing.

John Wyatt

John Wyatt is a Protestant Christian author and professor of ethics and perinatology at University College London. He is known for his writing on bioethics and the sanctity of human life, particularly in the context of medical technology and end-of-life care.

Wyatt acknowledges that there is some confusion about when an embryo or foetus begins to be human, and that even early Christian thinkers had differing views. Whilst some argue that life begins at conception, St Augustine did not view an unformed embryo as a living soul. In more recent history, Professor Donald Mackay argued that a critical level of complexity was required in foetal development before it could be considered a *'conscious personal agency'*. Since embryo research could enable treatments that reduce suffering, it could be seen as a Christian duty.[11]

However, Wyatt argues that embryos should always be treated with respect and dignity as they have a clear genetic identity from conception. Whilst not all embryos will survive, he argued that we have a moral responsibility to treat each one as though it will. We must approach new human beings, including those whose humanity is ambiguous, with the belief that God has called them out of nothing into a personal being.

Wyatt maintains that Christian thinking places a great emphasis on our responsibility to care for vulnerable and defenceless human beings, even those who may appear different from us. The early embryo, being vulnerable, represents those to whom we owe a special duty of care and protection. Thus, we should vote in favour of their protection and against any form of research upon them, or even intentional

---

[11] See John Wyatt, *Matters of Life and Death* (IVP, 1998).

destruction. If there is any doubt about their moral status, we should err on the side of caution and choose to protect them.

He further argues that we cannot think of the embryo as simply an unborn baby or a biological mechanism, but as a new unique being that requires a new category of thought. The language we use should reflect his understanding, as it influences our moral discourse. To simply refer to it as an 'embryo' fails to differentiate between human embryos and any other type of embryos: under a microscope they are all very similar and it is easy to therefore think of them as having similar value. But if one refers to them as 'embryonic humans', the focus changes.

NON-RELIGIOUS RESPONSES

Peter Singer
Peter Singer is an Australian moral philosopher, preference utilitarian and bioethicist. He has written extensively on topics such as euthanasia, abortion, and global poverty, and is considered to be a controversial figure due to his views on the moral status of animals the value of human life.

Preference Utilitarians believe that rather than simply the principle of utility, we must also uphold the principle of autonomy, as follows:

- *Does this moral action achieve the greatest good for the greatest number of people?* (principle of utility)
And
- *Does this moral action reflect the explicit wishes of an interested person who is able to express their wishes?* (principle of autonomy)

Peter Singer believes that embryos do not have the same moral status as fully developed human beings because they cannot express moral autonomy, and therefore, their interests can be overridden by the interests of other beings. His viewpoint reflects his broader ethical framework, which prioritizes the reduction of suffering and the promotion of well-being.

In his book *Rethinking Life and Death*, Singer argues that early-stage embryos do not have consciousness or the ability to feel pain, and therefore, it is not morally wrong to destroy them. He states that embryos attain their value from people who want them, for example parents who are trying to create embryos for IVF. Beyond that, they do not yet have intrinsic value. Singer also opposes the Roman Catholic argument that there is a single 'moment' of conception, noting that the process of 'syngamy' takes up to 24 hours. Although he says that an embryo gains the status of human after 14 days, he still thinks we do not achieve full personhood until after birth.[12] He supports research on embryonic stem cells for medical purposes, but he also advocates for strict regulations to ensure that these practices are not abused. He is also critical of some of the ways in which embryos are treated and used, particularly in the context of assisted reproduction. He is opposed to practices such as sex selection and the creation of 'designer babies', as they could end up reinforcing social problems.

Simon Fishel

Simon Fishel is a British embryologist. When considering the potential 'life' of an early embryo, Fishel notes that in natural conception up to 70% of fertilised eggs never succeed in implanting in the uterus wall: considering something that has not implanted as a human means that the majority humans ever to exist have never been born. In recent years, Fishel has been one of the first embryologists to feed an embryo in vitro, enabling it to survive beyond the 6-day limit after an embryo would normally implant in the uterus wall.

He argues that embryo research has the potential to bring great good to the world, and that rather than focusing on moral concerns we should extend the legality of embryo research from 14 to 28 days. He argues that this will enable better understanding of genetics and human

---

[12] Peter Singer, *Rethinking Life and Death* (Oxford, 1994), 94-99.

disease and will enable great leaps forward in medicine in the future. As new technology and understanding is allowing scientists to approach the 14-day limit, he thinks extending it to 28 days is the next step, as it would allow study of the process of gastrulation and the early development of human systems. Although critics have questioned this due to the possibility of pain beyond 14 days, he points out that a 28-day embryo still bears little physical resemblance to a human. He says *'the benefits for medical research would be enormous... Certain tumours, developmental abnormalities, miscarriage: there could be a whole raft of issues in medical science that we could start to understand if we could carry out research on embryos that are up to 28 days old'*.[13]

Critics of Fishel's suggestions include Mary Warnock herself, who argued that 14 days was the best cut-off point to ensure no harm comes to potential lives.

DISCUSSION POINTS

1. John Wyatt argued that in terms of moral discourse, that the word 'embryo' should be seen as belonging to science, and that as ethicists the term 'embryonic human' is more helpful. To what extent do you agree with him?
2. Do you believe it is acceptable to store eggs and/or embryos indefinitely?
3. How far should we be allowed to take embryo research and designer babies?
4. Should the 14-day rule be increased to allow more research, or is that potentially harmful to meaningful beings?

---

[13] Simon Fishel, quoted in *The Guardian*, 4 December 2016: https://www.theguardian.com/society/2016/dec/04/row-over-allowing-research-on-28-day-embryos

4 ABORTION

Abortion, the deliberate termination of a pregnancy, is in the public eye at the moment due to the US Supreme Court ruling that allows individual states to ban abortions in 2022. Many see this as travelling in the wrong direction. But abortion is not fully decriminalised in the UK either. It was legally allowed in the UK in 1967, but only under certain strict conditions: the mother's life or physical or mental health is endangered, existing children will be put at risk, or the foetus has a high likelihood of severe disabilities when born. It is allowed up to 24 weeks gestation, or full term in case of disability or if the mother's life is in danger. These rules were put in place after a bill by David Steel, who pointed out the increasing problem of back-street illegal abortions and the dangers to women associated with them. In Scotland today, 99% of abortions are medical and involve taking two pills. As of 2017, they can be performed at home in early pregnancy. However, later abortions can be more complicated. Across the world, 41% of women live under strict abortion laws and an estimated 23,000 women dying each year from unsafe abortions.

History of abortion
Abortion and infanticide (the killing of newborn infants) were both relatively widespread in ancient cultures. Early Christians discouraged

infanticide and it was banned in the Roman Empire in 374 CE. Late-term abortions gradually began to be seen as having a similar negative moral status. However, people did not have a fixed definition of when life begins. Most ancient cultures that believed that body and soul are separate (known as dualism) thought that life begins at quickening or ensoulment: around 18 weeks gestation and associated with when the mother could feel a baby move. In Britain, abortion before 'quickening' may have always been a relatively common practice. In 1861, the Offences against the Person Act made all abortion strictly illegal in Britain, with a maximum sentence of life imprisonment. The only exception was if a woman's life was in danger. In practice, some very wealthy people paid gynaecologists to perform abortions under the radar, claiming that life was somehow at risk. However, back-street abortions also became increasingly commonplace. These were often performed in unsanitary conditions, and serious medical consequences could occur. In 1966, the Royal College of Obstetricians and Gynaecologists estimated that at least 14,600 abortions (possibly many more) were occurring each year, of which most were illegal. In 1967, at least 32 women died from the results of illegal abortions in the UK.

In 1966, David Steel presented his Private Member's Bill in the House of Commons. It did not establish the right or autonomy of women over their bodies, but was instead intended to combat the serious problems of illegal abortions by providing a safe and regulated way in which they could take place. This was passed into law in England, Wales and Scotland in 1967.

1967 Abortion Act (modified slightly 1990)

Abortion could take place if two doctors agreed in good faith, before 24 weeks' gestation, on one of the following grounds:

    a) The continuance of the pregnancy would involve risk to the life of the pregnant woman greater than if the pregnancy was terminated;

b) The termination is necessary to prevent grave permanent injury to the physical or mental health of the pregnant woman;

c) The continuance of the pregnancy would involve risk of injury to the physical or mental health of the pregnant woman, greater than if the pregnancy were terminated;

d) The continuance of the pregnancy would involve risk of injury to the physical or mental health of any existing child(ren) of the family of the pregnant woman, greater than if the pregnancy were terminated;

e) There is substantial risk that if the child were born it would suffer from such physical or mental abnormalities as to be seriously handicapped.

Abortions are allowed up to full term for grounds a) and e).

Alterations/modifications

As abortions have switched from surgical to medical, the need to be in a clinic has reduced. Since 2017, women have been allowed to take both abortion pills at home in Scotland. The legality of at-home abortions has helped reduce the average length of gestation at abortion and the problems attached to having an abortion in a clinic.

In 2022, MSP Gillian Mackay put forward a proposed bill to the Scottish Parliament with the aim of introducing 150-metre 'buffer zones' preventing the growing number of protests outside abortion clinics. This is still under consultation.

British abortion statistics (from 2021)

	England & Wales	Scotland
Total number of abortions	214,256	13,896
Abortion rate per 1,000 women	18.6	13.4
Medical abortions (%)	87	99
Surgical abortions (%)	13	1
Abortions before 10 weeks gestation (%)	89	90
Late abortions	565 (after 22 weeks)	125 (after 18 weeks)
Abortions due to physical or mental health of mother (%)	98	98
Abortions due to foetal abnormality	3,370	184
Ratio of babies born alive to foetuses aborted	3:1	4:1
Abortion rate in most deprived area per 1,000 women	27.5	18.9
Abortion rate in least deprived area per 1,000 women	12.6	9
Teen abortion rate	decreasing	decreasing
35+ abortion rate	increasing	increasing

As we can see, abortion rates are consistently lower in Scotland than in England and Wales. The vast majority of abortions are on the ground of the physical or mental health of the woman (ground c), are before 10 weeks, and are performed medically.[14]

The Republic of Ireland and Northern Ireland
Abortion was illegal until recently in both the Republic of Ireland and Northern Ireland. In 2018, 66.4% of people in Ireland voted to legalise abortion. The law followed soon afterwards. Abortions are now allowed on demand up to 12 weeks, or up to full term if the child is likely to die within 28 days of birth or if the mother's life is in danger. In 2018, the Westminster government ruled that the bans on equal marriage and abortion in Northern Ireland were unlawful and overturned them. In Northern Ireland, abortion is now also allowed up to 12 weeks gestation.

The USA
In 1973, the famous Roe vs Wade ruling allowed for a constitutional right to abortion. In June 2022, this was overturned by the conservative-dominated US Supreme Court with the support of 'pro-life' activists. The USA is now very divided on its abortion laws, with thirteen states including Texas and Alabama having effectively banned abortion, others introducing heavy restrictions, and others such as Oregon effectively allowing abortion on demand.[15]

---

[14] England and Wales abortion statistics can be found at https://www.gov.uk/government/statistics/abortion-statistics-for-england-and-wales-2021/abortion-statistics-england-and-wales-2021 . Scottish abortion statistics can be found at https://publichealthscotland.scot/publications/termination-of-pregnancy-statistics/termination-of-pregnancy-statistics-year-ending-december-2021/
[15] The Guttmacher Institute provides up to date information on abortion rules in different states in the USA. https://states.guttmacher.org/policies/south-dakota/abortion-policies

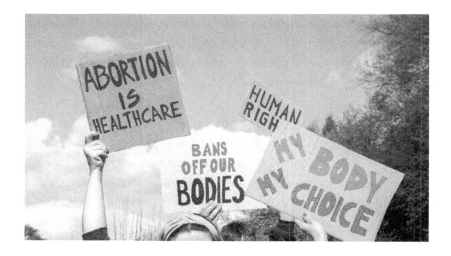

International abortion statistics

The general trend of abortion laws is that they have liberalised across the world over the last 25 years. However, in some countries such as Poland and the USA, laws are becoming stricter. [16]

While a majority of women live in countries where they can exercise a right to abortion, the inability of to access safe and legal abortion care impacts 700 million women of reproductive age. According to the World Health Organization, 23,000 women die due to unsafe abortions each year.

In China and Nepal, it is legal to abort on the grounds of gender. In Indonesia, parts of the Middle East and Japan, a husband's agreement is required in order for a woman to have an abortion.

The Guttmacher Institute estimates that around 121 unintended pregnancies occur around the world each year, with 61% ending in

---

[16] The Centre for Reproductive Rights has comprehensive information showing abortion statistics around the world. See https://maps.reproductiverights.org/worldabortionlaws for more information.

abortions. This is 73 million abortions each year.[17] An estimated 23 million unsafe/illegal abortions occur in Asia alone each year.

Abortion rates vary dramatically around the world.

Area	Abortion rate per thousand women per year
Australia and New Zealand	15
Europe & North America	17
South America & Sub-Saharan Africa	33
Eastern & South-East Asia	43
Central & Southern Asia	46
Western Asia & Northern Africa	53

As this information makes clear, wealthier countries tend to have much lower abortion rates. However, abortion rates are highest in Western Asia and Northern Africa, which are not the world's poorest areas. Countries that restrict abortion tend to have much higher unintended pregnancy rates (at 80 per thousand women compared to 58 per thousand women in countries where abortion is broadly legal), because they also tend to have less access to contraception and sexual health information. So even though a lower proportion of unintended pregnancies are aborted, their abortion rates are similar. Overall, abortion rates are similar (around 40 per thousand women) in countries where abortion is broadly legal and where it is prohibited altogether. This indicates that a ban on abortion does not lead to fewer abortions.

---

[17] The Guttmacher Institute: https://www.guttmacher.org/fact-sheet/induced-abortion-worldwide

Methods of abortion

The type of abortion given will depend on the gestation period at the time of termination. The earlier in a pregnancy, the less invasive the abortion has to be.

Gestation time	Method of Abortion	Details/Description
Before implantation (less than 6 days)	Intra-Uterine Device Morning after pill	These are often considered a type of contraception as they occur before pregnancy is known. However, they work between the time of conception and implantation.
Up to 12 weeks	Medical: two pills, normally 24 hours apart.	Mifepristone blocks the effects of progesterone, making the uterus less good for a foetus. Misoprostol causes the lining of the uterus to break down. Across Britain, these two pills may now be taken at home before 10-12 weeks.
12 to 20 weeks	Medical: two pills, normally 24 hours apart	This method still involves Mifepristone and Misoprostol but they will be taken in a clinic. This can take longer than an early medical abortion.
Up to 13 weeks	Surgical: vacuum aspiration	A local anaesthetic is given. A plastic suction tube is applied to the uterus to remove the

		foetus.
14 to 24 weeks	Surgical: dilation and evacuation	A general anaesthetic is given. The foetus is taken apart and removed from the uterus. *This method is not currently used in Scotland.*
After 20 weeks	Lethal injection	An injection is given to stop the heart of the foetus. It is later removed from the uterus. This is a more serious operation.

In Scotland, as we have seen, 99% of abortions are now medical and 90% are before 10 weeks. The classic gruesome images of surgical abortions do not reflect the realities of the procedure, as dilation and evacuation is not currently used in Scotland.

Alternatives to abortion
Improving contraception and sexual health
Hardly anyone argues that abortion is a positive or good thing. It would of course be better if unwanted pregnancies could be prevented in the first place. Pro-choice organisations such as the Guttmacher institute research abortion, contraception and sexual health and attempt to improve sexual health and education worldwide. As we have seen, improved access to contraception worldwide could dramatically decrease abortion rates.

Adoption
Historically, many adoptions took place in the UK but they were not legally regulated until the Adoption of Infants Act 1926. In the 1960s, the number of children put up for adoption was dramatically higher than now. The number was partly reduced by the availability of legal abortions, but also by birth control. In 1968, adoption numbers peaked

in England, with 24,800. The vast majority of these were born out of wedlock: it was deemed that unmarried mothers were generally not in a fit condition to bring up children alone. Numbers of children being put up for adoption decreased dramatically after the advent of abortion.

MORAL ISSUES

The rights of the embryo/foetus

The status of human life between conception and birth is obviously central to the abortion debate. Specifically, whether the foetus has a right to life and if so, at what point in the pregnancy does that right begin.

Opponents of abortion contend that the act of terminating a foetus is equivalent to committing murder against a human person. In 1869, Pope Pius IX declared that a foetus is a human person from the moment of conception, making abortion an act of homicide. Supporters of this view point to the presence of all the necessary genetic material at conception and the continued development from the fertilised egg to a fully-formed human being as evidence that the foetus is a person.

However, some critics argue that the fertilised egg is too dissimilar from anything that is conventionally recognised as a person to be classified as such. In her 1971 essay, 'A Defence of Abortion,' American Philosopher Judith Jarvis Thompson acknowledged that there is continuous growth in foetal development, but suggested that there is a point where it simply is not a human being. She likens the fertilised egg to an acorn, which, though it grows into an oak tree, is not an oak tree in and of itself. Similarly, a newly conceived clump of cells cannot be considered a person until it has some characteristics that are typical of people.[18]

---

[18] Judith Jarvis Thomson, 'A Defence of Abortion', *Philosophy and public affairs* 1 (1971).

Autonomy and whose rights come first?

Autonomy is the first principle of Biomedical Ethics, as laid out by US Ethicists Beauchamp and Childress in their seminal work on this subject.[19] The other three principles are beneficence, non-maleficence and judgement. The principle of the autonomy is the idea that a thinking individual should be able to make decisions about their own life. Judith Jarvis Thomson popularised this view. 'A Defence of Abortion' focuses on the idea that a woman should have the right to make decisions about her own body, and since the foetus is reliant on her body, she should have the right to say no to this when she does not want it. She created the 'violinist analogy' (see non-religious responses) to argue that one person does not have the right to infringe on another person's wellbeing and rights. Even if the foetus is considered a human person, it is not reasonable to demand that a woman carry it to term and potentially bring up the subsequent child. Thomson's focus is on women's rights and women having the ability to decide about their own futures. For Thomson, the woman's rights over her body supersede the foetus' right to life. Supporting Thomson's ideas, Situation Ethicist Joseph Fletcher stated that we should not be considering abortion as a moral wrong, but instead should be questioning the idea of *compulsory pregnancy*. He also described a pregnancy when not wanted as *'a venereal disease'*: something any woman should have the right to treat and cure herself of.[20]

Controversial Australian Preference Utilitarian Peter Singer argues that autonomy and rights are based on self-consciousness and the ability to think rationally. This includes any creature, human or not, with a sense of the self, but does not include unborn or newly born children or those who are severely disabled. Therefore, he argues that while women may have rights, unborn children do not. *'Killing them [infants], therefore, cannot be equated with killing normal human beings, or any other self-*

---

[19] See Tom Beauchamp & James Childress, *Principles of Biomedical Ethics* (Oxford, 1979).
[20] Joseph Fletcher, Humanhood (Prometheus, 1979), 138.

conscious beings. No infant - disabled or not - has as strong a claim to life as beings capable of seeing themselves as distinct entities existing over time'.[21]

However, opponents of abortion such as Roman Catholics argue that the foetus is also a vulnerable individual made in the image of God, and just because it is not able to express its own autonomy does not mean that it has no rights. They argue that the right of the baby to *live* takes precedent over the right of the woman to be *comfortable* or *happy*, as *life* is a more important right than *comfort* or *happiness*. They also argue that they do not deny women their rights but want to advocate alternative to abortion, such as refraining from sexual activity and adoption. British Christian Medical Ethicist John Wyatt argues that abortion laws can take women's rights away, for example when the fathers pressurise them into abortions that they do not really want and refuse to support their desire to be parents or take responsibility for their own actions.[22]

American legal philosopher Ronald Dworkin tries to find a middle ground here. He presents the idea of 'procreative autonomy'. He emphasises the rights to religious toleration, conscience and privacy. He notes that both pro-life and pro-choice advocates belief that life is sacred, but simply disagree on whose life should be prioritised and one what that sacredness should look like in practice. He also says that if a woman believes abortion is wrong, she should never be forced into it and should be allowed to put the rights of the unborn child first, but if she believes that abortion is acceptable and that she needs it in order to remain autonomous then she should have access to it. Likewise, no doctors should be forced to be involved in providing abortions and each

---

[21] Peter Singer, *Practical Ethics* (Cambridge University Press, 1979), 122-125.
[22] John Wyatt, 'Abortion in the modern world' (2019), available at: https://johnwyatt.com/2019/02/06/abortion-in-the-modern-world-the-current-realities/

individual should retain their autonomy.[23]

Ableism

As we have seen, the abortion law in the UK allows abortion up to full term in cases of severe disability. Although fewer than 2% of abortions are on these grounds, many disability rights activists, as well as opponents of abortion, argue that this is discriminating against foetuses with disabilities and therefore implying that their lives are less valuable. The definition of 'substantial risk' and 'seriously handicapped' in the wording of the law has also been called into question, and now functionally it often includes suspicion of a wide variety of disabilities from non-viable brain malformations to cleft palate.

This argument can be extended to the question of how open we should allow abortion to be. In parts of South Asia in particular, abortion for gender has been widely practised in the past, with people preferring boys to girls. If abortion is allowed completely on demand, isn't there a risk that it will put vulnerable people in more danger?

The pro-life organisation the Society for the Protection of Unborn Children (SPUC) compares pre-birth tests for Down's syndrome and other genetic disorders to the eugenics practiced in Nazi Germany. They note Department of Health documents announcing that genetic tests would save money on the upkeep of disabled children. *'Parents, as well as unborn babies, increasingly become victims of this sort of philosophy as the economic pressures on the health service increase and as tests for disabilities become more and more widely available'.*[24] John Wyatt discusses the discrimination felt by many disabled rights activists when women with disabled foetuses are routinely offered abortions. He argues from a compassionate Christian viewpoint that: *'There is accumulating evidence that health professionals consistently undervalue*

---

[23] Dworkin's view is examined by John Wyatt in *Matters of Life and Death* (IVP, 1998).
[24] SPUC, *Love your Unborn Neighbour*, 1994.

the lives of disabled, ex-premature adolescents compared with parents and with the individuals themselves.'[25] Wyatt argues that vulnerability and dependence are important human qualities and that discrimination against disabled people such as those with Down's Syndrome is an equivalent to racism: 'chromosomalism'. Several recent documentaries have explored whether current abortion laws led to discrimination against people with Downs Syndrome in particular.[26] In 2021, British disability rights activist Heidi Crowter attempted to reform the abortion law to introduce equality for those with disabilities, but her bid failed at the Supreme Court. In May 2023, she announced her plan to take this to the European Court of Human Rights. Many studies show that a higher proportion of people with Down's syndrome are happy with their lives than the general population, which can lead us to wonder 'what makes a life worth living'?

As medical research and technologies improve and we understand disabilities better, we are more able to treat and help people with disabilities than ever before. For instance, it is now possible to operate on some conditions such as spina bifida in-utero, dramatically improving quality of life, even though abortions are offered as an alternative to these conditions. Also, the lives of those with conditions such as Down's syndrome can be better than ever before, with better understanding of education and increased literacy rates and job opportunities. With these improvements, it could be argued that abortion on the grounds of disability becomes less necessary. Disability rights campaigners argue that even if term e) in the law is not removed, it should be clarified to state which conditions allow termination up to full term, as currently the same regulations are used to cover a wide range of conditions, including anencephaly, Down's syndrome, and cleft palate.

However, many pro-choice campaigners argue that it should be the

---

[25] John Wyatt, *Matters of Life and Death* (IVP, 1998).
[26] See in particular *A World Without Down's* (BBC, 2015) and *Disability and Abortion: the Hardest Choice* (ITV, 2022).

woman's decision whether she wants to parent a child who will be born with disabilities. This is not the same as discriminating against people once they are born but is simply showing that any disabling condition is not preferable when given the choice. They argue that a woman should have the right to decide what she feels she can cope with. Yet more critics point out that the information currently offered to women who discover their foetuses may have disabilities is not adequate for them to make informed decisions, so even if the law is not changed, the education about different disabilities should be improved.

In an extreme view, Peter Singer argues that infanticide should be an acceptable concomitant of abortion if society is to be consistent, and that people should not be forced to keep a severely disabled child if they do not feel able to, even after they are born. He also argues that life as a disabled person is proportionally less valuable than life as a non-disabled person: from this a logical conclusion is that disabled lives are less valuable. Likewise, he says that a foetus or baby that cannot yet express its preferences derives its value solely from those who care about it: once it is not wanted, it has lost its value. Singer has come under severe criticism from disabled rights activists, who also demonstrated in 1999 when he was made chair of Bioethics at Princeton University.

While many modern thinkers may find Singer's view on infanticide easy to dismiss as morally abhorrent, it does challenge us to articulate the moral difference between a full-term foetus with a disability and a pre-mature born baby with disabilities. This moral issue goes far beyond the clichéd pro-life versus pro-choice debates on this topic.

RELIGIOUS RESPONSES

The Roman Catholic Church
The Roman Catholic Church is the most famous traditional opponent of abortion in all forms, although today many Evangelical Christians in the

USA are also vehemently anti-abortion. The Catholic Church's ethical teachings are based on the idea that human life and personhood both begin at conception and that any taking of life is always wrong. The Catechism of Catholic Ethics states: *'Human life must be respected and protected absolutely from the moment of conception'*. However, the Bible does not directly mention when life begins. The main verses that are used in support of this are as follows:

From my mother's womb you have been my God. (Psalm 22:10)

You knit me together in my mother's womb. (Psalm 136:13)

Before I formed you in the womb I knew you, before you were born I set you apart. (Jeremiah 1:5)

In the New Testament Gospel of Luke, a touching story describes Mary the mother of Jesus meeting her cousin Elizabeth, mother of John the Baptist, when they were both still pregnant. Mary was still in the early stages of her pregnancy at this point. Elizabeth says that the foetus in her womb 'leaped for joy' when he heard Mary speaking, because he knew that Mary was carrying the Messiah. Many Catholics interpret this to mean that John was already sentient and capable of strong emotions as a foetus. Likewise, Jesus was already a recognisable person, already himself, and already the Messiah, even though he was still an embryo.[27]

---

[27] See the Bible, Luke 1:39-56.

The story of the incarnation of Jesus is another important moment in Catholic theology of the beginning of life. They argue that Jesus was incarnated (made flesh) by the Holy Spirit at the moment the Angel Gabriel spoke to Mary. This was the time that conception happened. From this moment, Mary was carrying Jesus, who was both fully human and fully God and destined to be the saviour of the world. He was not given his Jesus-ness at some later point. Therefore, they say, if Jesus was fully human from the moment of his conception, then all humans are.

Even within the Catholic Church, these teachings have not always been certain. Most early Christian thinkers, such as St Augustine, were influenced by Plato's teaching that the body and soul were separate. These thinkers argued that 'ensoulment' happens at a certain point during pregnancy (although they disagreed on when). Before ensoulment, the foetus could be seen as 'unformed'. It only became a human life, a person, once it was 'formed'. Augustine repeatedly said that *'the death of an unformed foetus was not homicide'*.[28] In the early church, early abortion was only seen as a problem if a woman was getting an abortion to conceal sexual sins such as adultery. However, the early church generally saw abortion as some sort of sin or crime,

---

[28] Beverly Wilding Harrison, 'Selected Early Catholic Teaching on Abortion', in *T&T Clark reader in Abortion and Religion*, eds. Rebecca Todd Peters and Margaret D. Kamitsuka (Bloomsbury, 2023).

even though it was not as serious as murder. The Roman Catholic Church only officially said all abortion was wrong from conception in 1869.

Many Roman Catholic organisations also aim to help promote alternatives to abortion. The Cardinal Winning centre in Glasgow offers practical solutions to people facing crisis pregnancies, including advice, nappies and baby care facilities, and emotional support. Mother Teresa, the Albanian Catholic nun who worked for many years with street children in India, said *'Please don't kill the child. I want the child. Please give me the child. I am willing to accept any child that would have been aborted'*. Traditionally, Catholic orphanages around the world have taken in thousands of children whose parents are unable to look after them.

A liberal Christian perspective
Many Christians, including some Roman Catholics, strongly disagree with the official Roman Catholic doctrine. In the USA, where abortion is a significant political issue, 65% of white evangelical Protestants, 66% of Mormons and 68% of Jehovah's witnesses think that abortion should be illegal in most or all cases. However, only 45% of black evangelical Protestants and 42% of white Catholics think about should be mostly illegal. In contrast, only 23% of Jews, 38% of Muslims, and 22% of people with no religion think abortion should be mostly illegal.

As we can see, abortion is a significant political issue in the USA. There is also a divide in terms of race. Many liberal Christians see restricting abortion as a further oppression of people of colour and people living in poverty. Liberal Christian thinker Shane Claiborne states that *'white Christians in America are the only demographic that consistently views abortion as either their only priority or their top priority... it is much farther down the priority list for most born again Christians of colour'*.[29]

---

[29] Shane Claiborne, *Rethinking Life* (Zondervan, 2023), 204.

Most liberal Christians support abortion. These choose to emphasise the needs of women as born humans, and the love that Jesus called people to show to others in vulnerable and needy situations. They see banning abortion as a form of social control. American Christian feminist philosopher Margaret D. Kamitsuka says *'there are at least four reasons why abortion should not be seen as an ipso facto intentional sin'*:[30]

1) There is no basis for abortion as a sin in Christian theology. Abortion was not deemed a sin in church law until the Middle Ages, and even then it was only for the 'formed' foetus (after supposed ensoulment at about 18 weeks). Kamitsuka says we can see a foetus as a living being and a potential person, but not yet a fully formed person. Although an abortion is a type of death, she says that this is a death *'without malice'*, so is not the same as murder.
2) Abortion is not the denial of a person's value. Instead, we can see it as a woman acknowledging that she feels unable to take on the caring, nurturing role for this being.
3) Abortion is not a sin against God. Even if it is, it is less sinful than either the judgement or the forced pregnancy called for by pro-life protestors.
4) It is not a sin to survive, and the need for abortion is part of the survival of many women. Kamitsuka says that *'in some situations, what a woman deems as necessary for survival... may mean she loses her so-called innocence in lieu of a wise course of action. This kind of survival cannot be appropriately labelled sin'*.

NON-RELIGIOUS RESPONSES

Judith Jarvis Thomson

Feminist American philosopher Thomson wrote her essay *In Defence of*

---

[30] See Margaret D. Kamitsuka, 'Contesting abortion as sin', in *T&T Clark reader in Abortion and religion*, ed. Rebecca Todd Peters & Margaret D. Kamitsuka (Bloomsbury, 2023).

Abortion in 1971, after abortion had been legalised under certain conditions in the UK, but before Roe vs Wade had established the constitutional right to abortion for American women. In her essay, she argued that the humanity or otherwise of the foetus was not relevant to the discussion, except perhaps in cases of late-term abortions after viability, which could be problematic. In most cases, she said, the rights of the woman should come first. Her violinist analogy asked her readers to imagine that they woke one morning to find they had been kidnapped by the Society of Music Lovers because they were the only person who could save the life of a famous violinist with a kidney disorder. To do this, they had to remain 'plugged into' him for nine months, or perhaps nineteen years, and not move or do anything else in this time. Thomson argued that someone could accept this status, and this self-sacrifice would make her perhaps a 'good Samaritan'. However, she said any person would be equally within their rights to refuse this state, object to being taken against their will, and demand that they be 'unplugged' from the violinist and allowed to continue with their lives. One can do this without being wrong or violating a moral code and still be a 'minimally decent Samaritan'. To choose not to remain plugged into the violinist does not make someone an awful person deserving of judgement. Thomson says it is exactly the same with pregnancy. Even if a foetus could be said to have the same rights as a born human being, this would still not give it the right to demand its mother's body as a dwelling place if she was not willing to loan it.

This is a very powerful discussion and has been influential for decades. However, it is open to some criticisms. Various thinkers have pointed out that unplugging oneself from a violinist is a non-violent act, whereas actively killing a foetus through whatever means is an inherently violent act.[31] Also, the analogy lends itself to various futuristic moral dilemmas. If an alternative method of treating the violinist became possible, wouldn't this be preferable to simply allowing him to die? In the same way, if an artificial uterus allowed the development of a foetus outside

---

[31] For example, see David Albert Jones' argument in *Dialogue* 40 (2013), 34.

of the womb, would it be morally preferable to transfer all unwanted foetuses to an artificial uterus rather than allowing them to die?

Thomson uses other analogies in her essay too. She argues that if seeds fly in through an open window of a room, someone has the right to remove them from their carpet to prevent them from growing into trees and destroying her house. In the same way, she says that someone should be able to remove an unwanted embryo that is effectively still a seed.

TASK

Look at the charts below and consider the different statements. How far do the different thinkers we have looked at agree with these statements? What do you think about them? The religious view has been completed for you. Now map the non-religious views of Judith Jarvis Thomson and Peter Singer, and your own view, in the other two charts.

Religious views of abortion

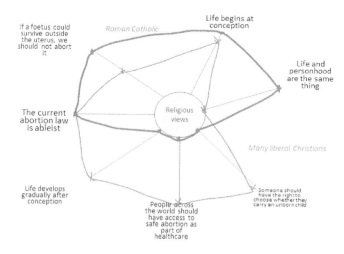

Non-religious views (please complete with Judith Jarvis Thomson and Peter Singer)

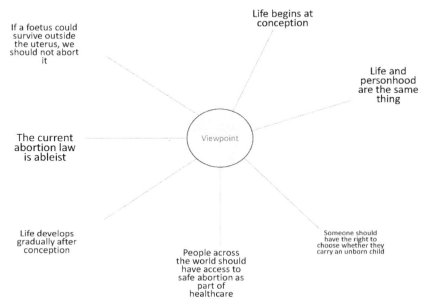

Your view (please complete)

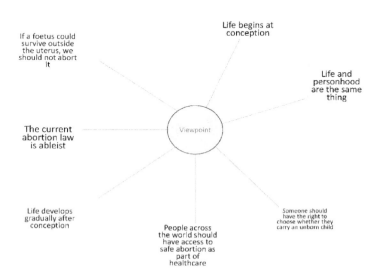

DISCUSSION POINTS

1. *Christian Ethicist John Wyatt describes a thought-provoking scenario, which he presents as a moral paradox with the current system, about the beginning of life and viability. A woman in one hospital room, let's say at 23 weeks' gestation, is in premature labour and doctors are fighting to save the life of her child. In the neighbouring room, another woman, also at 23 weeks' gestation, is undergoing a late-term abortion and doctors are aiming to ensure her foetus does not survive birth. If we switched this scenario to a disabled foetus, both women could be 32 weeks pregnant.*

How would you respond to this? Is it acceptable that abortion can sometimes take place after viability? Is a person's value derived from their ability to survive, or from being wanted by others, or from something more innate to humanity?

2. What is the most important moral consideration in abortion decisions: personhood, autonomy or disability?

3. Do abortions discriminate against people with disabilities?

DISCUSSION TASK: A DAY AT THE CLINIC

Look at this cartoon, showing seven women who want an abortion.

a) Should all of these people be offered abortions, or could other alternatives be more appropriate? Is more information needed here?

b) Should the stage of pregnancy affect whether they are offered an abortion?

c) How might the different religious and non-religious thinkers we have looked at respond to these requests for abortion?

d) What are the protestors doing? Why? What should their rights be? Should there be a buffer zone around the clinic?

e) According to the current law, under what ground would these people be offered abortions?

f) Does the current law adequately reflect the reasons that people want abortions?

g) Should the abortion law in Scotland be changed? If so, how?

5 ORGAN TRANSPLANTS

An organ transplant is a medical procedure to give a person with organ failure (the recipient) an organ from another person (the donor). The most common organ transplants are kidney, liver, heart, lung, and pancreas transplants. Tissues that can be transplanted include bone, cornea, skin, and heart valves. Transplants can be after brain death, after circulatory death, or for some organs while a donor is still alive.

People may need transplants when their organs or tissues are no longer functioning properly due to disease, injury, or congenital defect. The success of organ transplants depends on various factors, including the compatibility of the donor and recipient, the quality of the organ or tissue, and the recipient's overall health. Organ transplants significantly improve the quality of life and survival rates of patients with organ failure.

In Scotland, the 2006 Human Tissue Act regulated organ transplants and outlawed the buying and selling of organs. In 2021, the Human Tissue (Authorisation) Act introduced an 'opt-out' system for organ transplants, where Scottish residents over the age of 16 are presumed to want to donate their organs upon death unless they have stated otherwise.

There are currently not enough organs to go around and each year roughly 10% of people on the transplant list die while waiting for an organ: who should receive organs is an important question of distributive justice. Only 1% of people die in a way that makes their organs suitable for transplant, contributing to this shortage.

Across the world, the illegal organ trade is a big problem, with around 10% of organ transplants worldwide the result of illegal trafficking. This can lead to the exploitation and even murder of vulnerable people.

Transplant statistics (from 2022-2023)[32]

Number of...	UK	Scotland
People on transplant list	6,950	539
Organ transplants in last year	4,491	389
Transplants after death	3,575	295
Living donations	916	94
People who have opted out	2,484,818	177,238

MORAL ISSUES

- How should consent around organ transplants work?
- Is it acceptable to take organs from dead bodies, with or without their consent?
- Is 'presumed consent' ethically acceptable?
- Can organ sales ever be acceptable?
- How can we make fair decisions about distributing organs?
- Are there some lifestyle choices that mean you should be excluded from receiving an organ transplant?

---

[32] See NHS UK website: https://www.organdonation.nhs.uk/helping-you-to-decide/about-organ-donation/statistics-about-organ-donation/

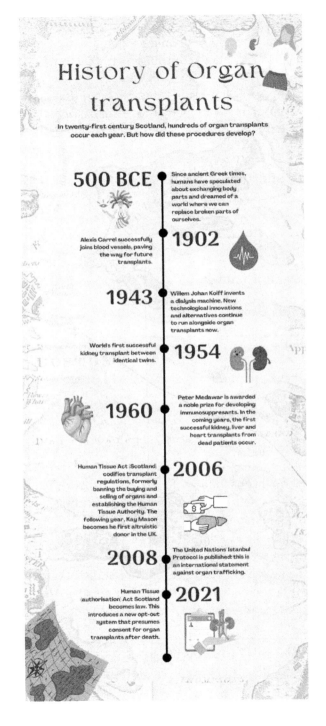

History of Organ transplants

In twenty-first century Scotland, hundreds of organ transplants occur each year. But how did these procedures develop?

500 BCE — Since ancient Greek times, humans have speculated about exchanging body parts and dreamed of a world where we can replace broken parts of ourselves.

Alexis Carrel successfully joins blood vessels, paving the way for future transplants. — **1902**

1943 — Willem Johan Kolff invents a dialysis machine. New technological innovations and alternatives continue to run alongside organ transplants now.

World's first successful kidney transplant between identical twins. — **1954**

1960 — Peter Medawar is awarded a noble prize for developing immunosuppresants. In the coming years, the first successful kidney, liver and heart transplants from dead patients occur.

Human Tissue Act (Scotland) codifies transplant regulations, formerly banning the buying and selling of organs and establishing the Human Tissue Authority. The following year, Kay Mason becomes he first altruistic donor in the UK. — **2006**

2008 — The United Nations Istanbul Protocol is published; this is an international statement against organ trafficking.

Human Tissue (authorisation) Act Scotland becomes law. This introduces a new opt-out system that presumes consent for organ transplants after death. — **2021**

6 ORGAN PROCUREMENT

Organ procurement means how we get organs such as kidneys, livers, and hearts for donation, and is regulated by the Human Tissue Authority (HTA). In March 2023 there were 6,950 people with organ failure waiting for transplants in the UK, including 539 in Scotland.[33] In 2021, an opt-out law was introduced in Scotland, meaning that everyone over the age of 16 is presumed to be an organ donor when they die unless they have stated otherwise. The government hopes this will increase donor numbers. Living donation is when people donate to friends or family members. In altruistic donations, people donate organs to those they have never met. Worldwide, the illegal organ trade leads to organs thefts and sales, which exploit vulnerable people.

Human Tissue (Scotland) Act (2006)
This act stated that organs would be regulated by the Human Tissue Authority (HTA). It made organ sales punishable by up to three years in

---

[33] For this and other statistics about organ donation in Scotland and across the UK, see the NHS UK website: https://www.organdonation.nhs.uk/helping-you-to-decide/about-organ-donation/statistics-about-organ-donation/.

prison, and made it illegal to take an organ from a live person without properly informed consent. It also allowed children aged 12 or over to provide written consent for organ donation, which must be taken into account by their relatives.

Human Tissue Authorisation (Scotland) Act (2021)
A new 'opt-out' act was passed by the Scottish Parliament in 2019 and came into law in March 2021.

A register is kept (not open to the public) with a list of people who have refused consent. An adult may make a declaration that they do not allow the use of any of their body parts after death. This should be sent to the register. Alternatively, with evidence, next of kin may show that the adult's most recent intention was that their organs should not be donated.

Unless they have made an opt-out declaration, an adult is deemed to have authorised the removal and use of a part of their body for transplantation after their death. If possible, a health worker must take reasonable steps before death to ensure that the patient is given the chance to express an opinion about organ donation and further treatment.

TYPES OF DONATION

Living donations
This is where a live donor donates an organ, most often a kidney, to a recipient. In this procedure, one kidney is removed from the donor and placed into the recipient with non-functioning kidneys. The recipient will need to take immunosuppressants for the rest of their life and there is a chance of rejection, but this procedure can dramatically extend life (by an average of 15-20 years) and is far preferable to kidney dialysis. The donor has a slight chance of complications and will need time off work. Problems could arise if they developed a kidney condition of their

own in the future. In the UK, there is a strong emphasis on aftercare for these donors. In Scotland, there were 94 living donations in 2022-3, with 916 across the UK.

Directed
This is when the donor and the recipient know each other. They may be family members or friends and are a close organ match.

Altruistic non-directed
This is when the donor and the recipient do not know each other. The donor could want to give a kidney away in the hope that they might start a chain and their own loved one, for whom they are not a match, will receive a kidney too. Alternatively, there may be a wide range of reasons why a person wants to donate their kidney to a stranger.

Living donations have a slightly higher success rate than donations after death, but they are much more restricted in scope.

Donations after death
Most organ donations (around 70-80%) occur after death. A donor's organs are checked and then matched with potential recipients. Up to ten organs can be retrieved from a single donor, potentially saving multiple lives. There were 295 transplants after death in Scotland from 2022-3, and about 3,575 in the UK as a whole.

Donation after Circulatory Death (DCD)
This is where the heart has stopped beating before donations occur.

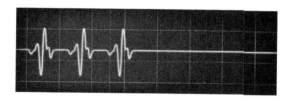

Donation after Brain Death (DBD)

In this procedure, the brain stem is deemed to be dead and the donor will not recover, but their heart is kept beating, often artificially, in order to preserve organ function.

DBD versus DCD

A slightly higher proportion of donors are after brain death rather than circulatory death. After brain death, it is easier to retrieve organs with an average of 3.4 organs retrieved per donor for DBD compared to 2.6 for DBD. However, some thinkers are concerned that as DBD is removing a donor's organs while their heart is still beating, this is mutilating a living body and causing death when there could still be a slim chance of recovery.

MORAL ISSUES

The integrity of the body

Many traditional theists believe that a body, even after death, has a level of integrity and importance. This leads some religious believers to reject organ transplants altogether. This includes followers of Shinto, Jehovah's Witnesses and some Muslims. The Old Testament contains the verse *'be sure you do not eat the blood, because the blood is the life'* (Leviticus 17:4). While even Orthodox Jews take this to mean refrain from eating food with blood, for Jehovah's Witnesses this means that any kind of blood or organ transfusion is problematic. In Shinto, injuring a dead body is a serious crime, as dead bodies are revered and considered powerful. In Islam, the body is seen as *'anamah'*, or in trust from God. The Hanafi school argues that a dead body must be buried, and the Maliki school says *'it is impermissible to treat the body by utilising anything that is regarded as forbidden in the same way as it is forbidden for one who is on the verge of starvation to consume human flesh'*[34].

---

[34] Abul Fadl Mohsin Ebrahim, *Organ Transplantation* (The Islamic Foundation, 2001).

Others, such as conservative Christian thinker Gilbert Meilaender, believe that while organ donation can have benefits in some cases, we should still pay close attention to the integrity of the body. We should not always do what science makes possible and sometimes we should question whether an organ transplant it the most appropriate form of action: *'if we learn to regard our bodies simply as collections of organs potentially useful to others… we are in danger of losing any close connection between the person and the body'*. He goes on to consider Leon Kass's comparison of organ transplants to *'a noble form of cannibalism'*: inherently problematic and only potentially permissible in extreme situations.[35]

However, many Christians see organ transplantation as a great moral good that overrides concerns about bodily integrity. Roman Catholic leader Pope John Paul II stated that through organ transplants, *'man has found a way to give of himself, of his blood and of his body, so that others may continue to live'*. He also says *'by analogy with Christ's Paschal Mystery [the crucifixion], in dying death is somehow overcome with life'*.[36] Former Archbishop of Canterbury Rowan Williams describes organ transplants as showing *'the willingness of countless men, women and children to think and act selflessly'* and describes organ donors as *'a sign of hope and an inspiration to all of us'*.[37] For both of these thinkers, the high moral good promoted by organ transplants is more important than concerns about the integrity of bodies. By comparing organ donation to sacrifice, both thinkers also suggest that to give an organ is to become sacrificial in the same way as Jesus: without being able to replicate his self-giving crucifixion, the selflessness of becoming a donor

---

[35] Gilbert Meilaender, *Bioethics: A Primer for Christians* (Eerdmans, 1996), 91.

[36] See John Paul II's address to participants of the first international congress of the society of organ sharing, 1991: https://www.vatican.va/content/john-paul-ii/en/speeches/1991/june/documents/hf_jp-ii_spe_19910620_trapianti.html

[37] Quoted from Roman Williams in a commemoration service at Ely Cathedral, 2017: https://www.cambridge-news.co.uk/news/health/rowan-williams-cambridge-organ-donor-13003248

takes one step towards his sacrificial attitude.

Some thinkers such as Situation Ethicist Joseph Fletcher argue that traditional religious views about funerals and the importance of bodies can cause harm by preventing us from using bodies to help others. Fletcher describes a *'body taboo'*, which *'adversely affects not only transplants but medical knowledge and education'*. He is deeply critical of those who use religion as an excuse not to donate organs, describing funerals and cremations as *'acts of callous indifference'* and saying *'we are prodigally wasteful in our funerary practices and stupidly selfish in our use of vital organs while we live and even more so when we die'*.[38] Humanists agree with this idea, with Jamie Theakston stated that *'we can't take our organs with us when we die... organ donation is one of the easiest, kindest things you can ever do'*.[39]

Today, 54% of people in Scotland have voluntarily opted in to donating their organs. However, the idea of consent and donating organs upon death remains taboo in many areas of the world, leading to more dramatic organ shortages in many Muslim-majority and socially conservative countries. The World Health Organisation says, *'If we are prepared to receive a transplant should we need one, then we should be ready to give'*.

---

[38] Fletcher, Joseph, *Humanhood* (Prometheus, 1979), 65-71.
[39] See the Humanist view of Organ Transplants at https://humanism.org.uk/campaigns/public-ethical-issues/organ-donation/.

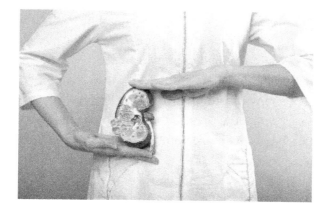

Consent and the opt-out system

Humanists campaigned to introduce the opt-out system. They quote the statistic that three people on the organ transplant list die each day while waiting for treatment, and argue that respect for the dead should not give *'any reason to object to allowing a deceased person's organs being used to help others, except where the deceased has expressed a contrary wish'*. They campaigned for the new laws, emphasising that the opt-out system presuming consent *'increases the number of organs available for transplant, saving lives'*.

However, critics of the 2021 opt-out law argue that it goes against our autonomy. Many Roman Catholics have expressed concern at the opt-out law, arguing that assuming people being forced to donate their organs takes away from the moral good of the act. Deontologists also argue that presuming consent for an organ transplant is simply using people as a means to an end.

Preference Utilitarians including Julian Savulescu and William Isdale are also concerned about the opt-out law, arguing that taking someone's organs without their explicit consent fails to promote altruistic ethical action and could go against people's preferences or autonomy.[40]

---

[40] Julian Savulescu and William Isdale, 'Three Ethical ways to increase organ donation in Australia', *The Conversation*, 3 June 2015.

However, a counter-argument is that we do not need to consent to something if we are dead and that the new law allows people to opt-out if they do not consent for their organs to be used.

The opt-out law is an interesting case where Preference Utilitarians and Roman Catholics agree and oppose the new law on the basis of autonomy. But if it will increase numbers of organ donations, does it really matter?

Buying organs

In the UK and most other countries (with the exception of Iran), buying and selling organs is illegal, and as we have seen it is the World Health Organisation's official policy to try to stop organ trafficking as it violates dignity. However, international organ trafficking rates have increased dramatically during Covid, putting vulnerable groups even more at risk. Some countries with poor human rights records such as China are suspected of harvesting organs from living 'donors', including political and religious prisoners, involuntarily. The World Health Organisation estimates that 10% of all organ transplants are illegally trafficked and that 10,000 kidneys are traded worldwide on the black market annually. Many people are concerned about people being commodified for parts, and how this affects the poorest, most vulnerable people the most. In 2008, the Istanbul Protocol stated that 'transplant tourism' and 'organ trafficking' were growing problems and declared that these practices *'violate the principles of equity, justice and respect for human dignity and should be prohibited'*. The World Health Organization has officially endorsed this protocol, meaning they support it and aim to ban the buying and selling of organs worldwide.[41] Many philosophers and ethicists agree that there are serious problems with selling organs: Soren Holm states that selling organs is exploitative if the donor *'is in a*

---

https://theconversation.com/three-ethical-ways-to-increase-organ-donation-in-australia-42744

[41] See the Istanbul Protocol here:
https://www.ohchr.org/en/publications/policy-and-methodological-publications/istanbul-protocol-manual-effective-0

severely materially or socially deprived situation'.[42] Samuel Kerstein argues that the existence of any sort of organ market could *'harm poor people'*[43] and Katrina Bramstedt says that allowing organ sales could create an *'economic class war'* in which the rich bought organs from the poor.[44]

However, some thinkers argue that having a controlled market for buying and selling could be an effective way to protect people from exploitation. Sean Columb is an Irish researcher who has interviewed people affected by organ trafficking. He notes that harsh penalties for organ traffickers in Egypt are forcing the practice further underground and making things more dangerous. He also notes that people selling organs voluntarily is their own decision, and that preventing people from doing this simply because they are poor is problematic too. He describes cultural factors that lead to the problem of finding donors, and says that most donors *'require payment'*, and that many transplant coordinators he has worked with in Egypt consider it *'unethical not to pay a donor'*. Many of these donors are migrants who are trapped in poverty, unable to work in Egypt, and feel under pressure to send money home to their families. Here, he describes organ trading as *'a pragmatic decision based on local realities'*. He also states that the fact organ sales are illegal drives the practice underground and leads to the worst forms of exploitation and organ theft that we hear about in the media. He states that the introduction of a *'fixed incentive determined by the state'* would help to protect vulnerable donors from being exploited.

---

[42] Soren Holm, 'The Role of Informed Consent in Genetic Experimentation', in *Blackwell Companion to Genethics*, eds. Justine Burley & John Harris (2002), 85.
[43] Samuel Kerstein, 'Is it Ethical to Purchase Human Organs?', *The Guardian*, 29 June 2016:
https://www.theguardian.com/commentisfree/2016/jun/29/purchase-human-organs-kidney-wait-list-ethics
[44] Katrina Bramstedt, 'Buying and Selling Organs Would Create an Economic Class War', The New York Times, 21 August 2014:
https://www.nytimes.com/roomfordebate/2014/08/21/how-much-for-a-kidney/buying-and-selling-organs-would-create-an-economic-class-war

British feminist philosopher Janet Radcliffe Richards argues that organ selling should be allowed, even though it isn't an ideal option. She argues that presenting those in poverty purely as victims is demeaning, and that giving them the option of selling their kidney at least gives them an extra choice and does not remove any choices, whereas prohibiting it takes away choices from people. She also states that it is wrong to give choices to the rich but deny more important choices to the poor: 'if the rich who take up hang-gliding or mountaineering are regarded as entitled to judge their own risks, it is difficult to see why the poor, who propose to take lower risks for higher returns, should be regarded as so manifestly irrational as to need saving from themselves.' She also says that allowing organ sales could be an important way to increase donations: 'As long as people are dying for lack of organs... as long as both buyers and sellers suffer in the inevitable black market, the total prohibition of payment is almost certainly unjustified'.[45]

German academic Oliver Decker provides a counterargument for this, using a study of people in India who had sold their organs to show: 'Those who sold organs were no better off, and donors selling an organ certainly did not significantly improve their lot. The money received was immediately spent on food and clothing and quickly exhausted, so that despite the sale the donors continued to live in poverty. Thus although 86% of the donors studied had health problems after a transplant operation, they had no money to pay for treatment'. He states that the debate about organ sales can be characterised as 'free market arguments that are opposed by a Christian or Western derivation of human dignity'.[46]

This is a thorny argument: in a UK context, it is easy to criticise organ

---

[45] Janet Radcliffe Richards, 'Selling Organs, Gametes and Surrogacy Services', in Blackwell Guide to Medical Ethics, eds. Rosamund Rhodes, Leslie P. Francis, Anita Silvers (2007), 254-268.
[46] Oliver Decker, Commodified Bodies (Routledge, 2014), 31-32.

sales as deplorable and exploitative, but what if someone wants to sell their organ and sees it as their best option to escape extreme poverty? Couldn't criminalising it further be seen as a way of restricting their choices and forcing people to resort to dangerous illegal transplants, for which they may not even receive remuneration?

Alternatives to organ procurement

Organ procurement is a good thing and saves many lives, but alternatives could be even better, more reliable and more readily available. Technology in this area is developing quickly, and these are just a few recent examples.

Mechanical/synthetic organs

Mechanical organs are becoming increasingly complex and reliable with advances in technology. In 2011, a cancer patient was given an artificial trachea, but the surgeon Paulo Macchiarini was later discredited and most of his patients died. However, with advances such as 3D printing, artificial organs are becoming closer to reality. Mechanical heart pumps can now be carried in a backpack or similar to enable patients with heart failure to live active lives.

Xenotransplantation (animal organ transplantation)

This is transplantation from an animal into a human. In the past, there have often tended to be rejection issues with xenotransplantation, but genetic engineering is making it a more viable alternative for the future. Animals can now be used to grow human or human-like organs for transplantation. The world's first successful kidney transplant from pig to human occurred in October 2021, and in 2022 David Bennett survived for two months after receiving a pig heart transplant.

Organs grown through cloning/genetic engineering

Many scientists are also experimenting with growing organs from stem cell or other tissues, without the need for a host body. In 2019, a new technology was developed involving stem cells grown from an individual. This could 'beat' for their own heart. As synthetic 'meat' can now be grown in a lab, it seems only a matter of time until organs and other body parts can too. Various science fiction stories such as *Never Let me Go* and *The Island* have explored the idea of creating cloned humans in order to farm organs from them, but this tends to raise considerable moral objections.

RELIGIOUS RESPONSES

The Roman Catholic Church

Christians traditionally placed great importance in any body, living or dead. In the Bible, St Paul wrote: *'Your body is a temple of the Holy Spirit within you which you have from God'* (1 Corinthians 6:19). Most Christian traditions had religious funeral rites, including the need for a sacred burial ground. This was partly due to beliefs about resurrection, but also to show respect for humanity. Some Christian thinkers still have reservations about transplants from dead donors on this basis, although as we have seen the Church now officially endorses organ transplants and sees them as a moral good in the appropriate context.

Most Christians argue that the principle of treating corpses respectfully is overridden by the commandment: *'Love your neighbour as yourself'* (Mark 10:31). Christians believe that Jesus led by example, healing people's illnesses and disabilities on many occasions. We should make and take every opportunity to help people.

However, the Roman Catholic Church does have reservations about organ transplantation and ableism. They are concerned that greater rates of transplantation will lead to the removal of organs from anencephalic infants (this is a condition where the brain has not properly developed, which will prevent life from continuing), people in a persistent vegetative state and people with severe disabilities, thus violating the right to life. They state that causing death by removing organs from such people would be morally equivalent to murder. They are concerned about the definition of death, arguing that organs *'may not be removed until after death has taken place'*. This means that DBD can be controversial for Roman Catholics if the heart is still beating.

For donation after death, they state that informed consent must have been received: an opt-out system takes away the moral good of the act. For living donations, they insist that *'the surgical mutilation of a donor for the good of the recipient must not seriously impair or destroy bodily functions or beauty of the donor'*. They also state that *'One may intend to sacrifice an organ for the sake of another, but one also has the responsibility for the integrity of one's body'*. This means that living donations are not morally acceptable if they are harmful to the donor.[47]

They also state that organ transplants are only morally acceptable within the context of informed consent. So organ donation is a high moral good for Roman Catholics, but only when it is done with no financial benefit, coercion, potential harm to a living donor, or ambiguity about the moral status of a donor.

Islamic responses

Opinion within Islam is split on this topic. Many Muslim-majority countries have cultural barriers to organ transplants and a strong emphasis on the integrity of the body and the need to perform quick burials after death to secure a place in the afterlife. Muslims agree on the following basic principles:

- Our organs don't belong to us, but to God. They are lent to us in trust (*amanah*) from God.
- Since our organs belong to God, not us, it is always wrong to buy and sell them, or gain in any way from giving our organs away.

---

[47] 'Play it Again Organ Donation', Lay Witness Magazine (2001): https://www.catholiceducation.org/en/science/ethical-issues/play-it-again-organ-donation.html

- All humans are equal and bodies, both living and dead, should always be treated with dignity and respect.

The Hanafi school is strongly against organ transplantation, saying that you have to bury a human, rather than use any part of them in treatment or sell any part of them. It is also strongly against xenotransplantation, stating that it is forbidden to derive any form of benefit from, for example, pigs. The Maliki school compares organ transplantation to cannibalism to demonstrate that it is always forbidden. These schools support their beliefs with the following Hadiths, attributed to the Prophet Muhammad: *'Your life and your property and your honour are sacred until you meet your* Lord'; *'breaking the bone of a dead person is equal in sinfulness and aggression to breaking it while a person is alive'*; *'Allah created the disease and also the cure and for every disease he has provided a cure'. So treat yourselves with medicines, but do not treat yourselves with prohibited things'*. As human bodies are seen as forbidden things, this is interpreted to mean that the Prophet thinks medicine is important, but doesn't see organ procurement as a valid form of medicine. Muslims are also encouraged in the hadiths to avoid what is doubtful, so if they are not sure about organ transplantation, it could be better to avoid it.

However, other Muslims point to the law of public welfare (Al-Maslahah) to argue that *'necessity makes the unlawful permissible'*. This means that we can excuse the 'mutilation' of a dead body if it will bring a greater benefit to people, for example through saving lives. Islamic law allows cutting open a dead person if they have swallowed something valuable like a diamond, to restore the diamond to the rightful honour. Organ donation that saves someone's life could be the equivalent of cutting a diamond out of a dead person. It will be of great benefit to the person who gets it back.

Even scholars who approve of organ transplants think that it should have certain conditions on it:

- It must be the only possible form of treatment in the situation.
- It must be relatively likely to succeed.
- It has full consent and understanding from both parties (both the dead donor or their relatives and the recipient).
- If possible, it is better to receive an organ from a Muslim donor, because they have been living a life that is halal.[48]

In terms of altruistic living donations, the Qur'an says people should *'help one another in righteousness and piety'*. (Qur'an 5:2) Giving an organ to someone who really needs it can be a wonderful act of altruism and kindness. However, it should only be done if it is the only form of treatment possible, it has full consent, if it is likely to succeed and if it will not result in the death of the donor.

NON-RELIGIOUS RESPONSES

Humanists
As we have seen, Humanists promote organ transplants as a high moral good and campaigned for the introduction of opt-out laws across the UK. As they do not believe in an afterlife or innate bodily integrity, they adopt the consequentialist stance that any practical use of body parts after death should be taken on unless someone has explicitly objected to this.

Although this seems logical if we acknowledge that our bodies are of no use after death, it raises some interesting emotional and moral issues. Does this mean they think a body should be used for any possible purpose after death? What if we discovered a way to turn human bodies into an effective fuel or foodstuff (as in the 1973 film *Soylent Green*)? Is there a danger of another slippery slope here?

---

[48] Ebrahim, Abul Fadl Mohsin, *Organ Transplantation* (Islamic Press, 2001), 49-59.

Preference Utilitarians

Although many Utilitarians may agree with the Humanist view of organ procurement and presumed consent, Preference Utilitarians are unhappy with the introduction of presumed consent. Their founding principles of utility and autonomy come into conflict here, because the most 'useful' thing is being done without someone's explicit consent. Julian Savulescu and William Isdale argue that presuming consent for organ donation does not promote altruistic ethical action and could lead to people having to give organs to help others against their preferences. However, they think that organ donation should be a moral obligation, saying: '*Because a single donor can provide organs and tissue that benefit up to 10 other people, to choose not to donate is to allow those individuals to unnecessarily die or continue to suffer.*'[49] They argue that the following three measures could help increase organ donations instead:

- preventing families from being able to withdraw consent when the patient has given consent;
- giving financial incentives for organ donation;
- giving other incentives for organ donation, e.g. priority on waiting lists.

They argue that greater education and more public discussions about organ donation would enable people to make their own decisions without making assumptions about their desire to donate.

---

[49] Julian Savulescu and William Isdale, 'Three Ethical ways to increase organ donation in Australia', *The Conversation* June 3 2015: https://theconversation.com/three-ethical-ways-to-increase-organ-donation-in-australia-42744

DISCUSSION POINTS

1. If a dead body no longer has integrity, why do we still treat it with reverence and respect?
2. Does explicit consent for a transplant matter?
3. Could buying an organ ever be acceptable? What if it was your own family member who might die without an immediate transplant?
4. Instead of focusing on increasing number of organs available for transplant, could developing reliable alternatives be a better use of our resources?
5. Is organ procurement a form of 'noble cannibalism'? Does it matter?

TASKS

- How far do the different thinkers and viewpoints you have seen in this chapter agree with these statements? Try to map them out in these charts (see below).
- What do you think? Create an alternative map for yourself as a way of developing your evaluation.

Religious views

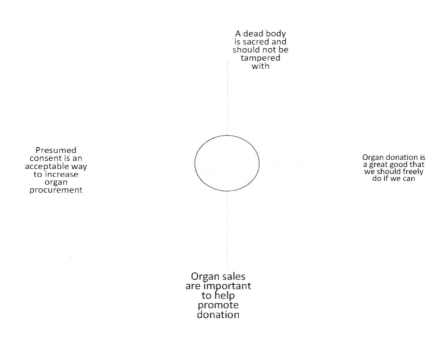

A dead body is sacred and should not be tampered with

Presumed consent is an acceptable way to increase organ procurement

Organ donation is a great good that we should freely do if we can

Organ sales are important to help promote donation

Non-religious views

A dead body
is sacred and
should not be
tampered
with

Presumed
consent is an
acceptable way
to increase
organ
procurement

Organ donation is
a great good that
we should freely
do if we can

Organ sales
are important
to help
promote
donation

My views

A dead body
is sacred and
should not be
tampered
with

Presumed
consent is an
acceptable way
to increase
organ
procurement

Organ donation is
a great good that
we should freely
do if we can

Organ sales
are important
to help
promote
donation

7 ORGAN ALLOCATION

In 2022, mother Ami McLennan was told by Manchester Children's Hospital that her 17-year-old son William Verden would not be granted a life-saving kidney transplant due to his Autism, ADHD and learning difficulties. The trust ruled that William was incapable of understanding what would happen to him, could not consent to the treatment, and would be confused and distressed by needing prolonged hospital care after the operation. Ami refused to accept this ruling, arguing that her son deserved the same treatment as anyone else and that he had expressed a desire to live. She took the health board to court, where the judge ruled that William was eligible for a kidney transplant. In August 2022, he received a kidney from a dead donor. The transplant was a success, and although he is at risk of his kidney problem recurring, he now stands a chance of living a healthy life.

But was the health trust discriminating against William because of his disability, or was it just trying to make pragmatic decisions? When there are not enough organs to go around, should everyone still have an equal chance of getting one or should people who will make the 'best use' of them receive preferential treatment?

Definition

Organ allocation refers to who receives an organ transplant. There are more people on the organ waiting lists than there are organs available, with around 6,950 people currently on the list in the UK and thousands more temporarily suspended from the list due to ill health. In the UK, there is a strict non-discrimination policy to ensure equity for organ allocation, and priority is only allowed to be given based on who has been on the list for longest or who is in super-urgent need. But in practice, the situation is often more complicated, as the fact there are not enough organs to go around means that '*a decision to offer one patient a transplant may deny other a life-saving procedure*'. A number of factors can prevent someone from being placed on the transplant list in the first place, including medical or psychiatric comorbidity, ongoing alcohol or drug abuse that would jeopardise the success of the transplant, and poor general quality of life. However, it is difficult to ensure that these policies are fair.

Current laws and policies in the UK

As we have seen, the Human Tissue Act (Scotland) 2006 states that buying and selling organs is illegal and consent is always needed. The Human Tissue Authority (HTA) regulates donations, including organ allocation. In the UK, it is also illegal for doctors to discriminate when deciding who will get an organ. Once someone is on the organ transplant list, they are placed in priority according to how long they have been on the list, and whether they are in super-urgent need (meaning they might not survive more than 72 hours without a transplant). In practice, many patients become too ill to receive a transplant while they are on the 'transplant list', and are removed or temporarily suspended from lists. Around 10% of patients on the list die each year while waiting for an organ they will never receive.

The organ allocation policy in the UK is based on the principle of **equitable treatment**. Organs are allocated to patients according to agreed criteria. The UK-wide allocation procedures are designed to ensure that patients are treated fairly and the donated organs are allocated in an unbiased way based on the patient's clinical need and the importance of a range of factors, one of which may be achieving the closest possible match between donor and recipient. The organ allocation and selection document lists the specific policy that *'Restrict[s] the list so that those who are listed will have a reasonable expectation that they will receive a transplant'.* This aims to prevent disappointment, as listing everyone who needs an organ would mean that *'many listed patients will have no realistic chance of receiving a transplant'.*[50]

Specific allocation policies are slightly different for different organs. For example, someone is only placed on the list to receive a donated liver if it there is at least a 50% chance they will survive another 5 years after the operation. Assessment as to whether someone is suitable for an organ transplant is carried out by a multidisciplinary team.
The NHS policy document recognises that the process is competitive and *'a decision to offer one patient a transplant may deny another a life-saving procedure'* (NHS).

Even in an emergency transplant situation, the decision still needs to be made by more than one healthcare professional. Priority may not be given to private patients simply because they are able to pay, but the same principles of equity must apply as for other patients. You can't be on the organ transplant list in the UK and somewhere else at the same time. If no organs within the UK are available, international organ transplants are technically allowed, but only under strict procedures that ensure no money has exchanged hands.

Sometimes, if there is a danger the organ will be unusable, the organ may be allocated to someone nearer. The amount of time an organ is

---

[50] For the official NHS document explaining organ allocation procedures, see:
http://odt.nhs.uk/pdf/introduction_to_selection_and_allocation_policies.pdf

separate from the original donor and cooled before it is implanted in the patient is called the cold ischaemic time (CIT). This can be increased with new technologies such as machine perfusion.

However, there are ten factors that may also prevent someone from joining the transplant list, which can be seen as a utilitarian balance to an equity-based system. If any of these factors develop, they can also mean that someone is removed or suspended from the list.

1. **Age.** While discriminating on the grounds of age is not allowed, the 'benefit of transplantation to the patient' is considered, which could include their likely quality of life after transplantation.
2. **Alcohol use/abuse.** Depending on the organ (e.g. liver), continued alcohol use or abuse could make a successful transplant very unlikely.
3. **Illicit drug use.** This could increase the risk of infection and make a successful transplant less likely.
4. **Adherence/non-adherence.** Organ recipients will most likely need to take immuno-suppressants for the rest of their lives. If it is deemed unlikely that they will comply, they are less likely to be placed on the list.
5. **Medical comorbidity.** If a patient has other serious medical conditions, this could affect the likelihood of transplant success/survival.
6. **Psychiatric comorbidity.** If a patient has a serious psychiatric disease/condition, it may make them unsuitable for a transplant. This could also be associated with non-adherence.
7. **Malignancy (past or current).** If a patient has had malignant cancerous cells in the past, the use of immuno-suppressants could enable the cancer to return. It may not be appropriate in these circumstances.
8. **Quality of life.** Although this is a vague and subjective concept, practitioners will question whether current poor quality of life is likely to be corrected by organ transplantation. If not, transplantation may not be appropriate.

9. **Malnutrition**. If a patient is malnourished, it is less likely that transplantation and recovery will be successful.
10. **Need for multiple organ transplantation**. Patients may not meet the criteria for transplantation for every organ they need. A specific order of priority exists here.

An alternative way of distributing medical resources is through measures such as QALYs (quality adjusted life years). Each QALY represents one predicted year in perfect health. This creates a numerical calculation for each patient based on how much extra life the intervention or medical procedure would give them, and what the quality of this life would be. However, these are very controversial. Can a judgement of whether something is worthwhile really be put down to a time scale, and is it really possible to put a numerical value on the quality of someone's life? An organ allocation system based on QALYs would have very different outcomes from the current equity-based system. If QALYs were adopted as a system for organ donation, those patients who were youngest and with fewer complicating factors would always be the first to receive transplants.

MORAL ISSUES

Is organ allocation always a moral good?
Ultimately, we could ask whether organ allocation itself is the best use of medical resources. In many cases, it is a very expensive procedure that will prolong the lives of those who are already very ill. But even those who have received organs will still be life-limited and have to take immunosuppressants for the rest of their lives. Couldn't resources be better spent vaccinating children in poverty-stricken countries whose lives may otherwise be dramatically shortened? Welfare Utilitarians such as Tony Hope argue that this is something we need to consider carefully. If someone has significant co-morbidity (lots of other things wrong with them), there are always others who should receive organs first, so maybe they should be excluded altogether. This is not necessarily because their lives have less value, but simply because a

transplant is less likely to be of long-term benefit. Conservative Christian bioethicist Gilbert Meilaender suggests from a Christian perspective that sometimes we are obsessed with prolonging life and this is not always in someone's best interests. He says that sometimes we should *'decline to do what medical technology makes possible'* and that we shouldn't always live as if *'staying alive as long as possible always has the moral trump'*.[51]

Although Preference Utilitarian Peter Singer supports organ transplantation in principle, his idea that *'not all lives are of equal value'* encourages people to consider whether certain lives are really worth putting the effort into saving. However, this viewpoint is controversial. In January 2021, former Supreme Court Justice Lord Sumption made the news by telling a terminal cancer patient and presenter of *You, Me and the Big C* Deborah James that her life was 'less valuable' and she should not receive a Covid vaccine. He was strongly criticised, with human rights barrister Adam Wagner describing his comments as *'inhumane, almost grotesque'*.[52] Many Christians agree with Wagner that to deny anyone resources such as a vaccine or an organ transplant is to discriminate against them, and as we are all made in God's image we should all be given a chance. Medical technology has been developed using God-given skills and we should make the most of it.

As with other moral issues with organ allocation, this comes back to the question: should we give an organ to the person who needs it the most to survive or to the person who will have the most benefit from it?

How can we distribute limited resources fairly? Is equity always the best way?

---

[51] Gilbert Meilaender, *Bioethics: A Primer for Christians* (1996), 100.

[52] See Clea Skopeliti, 'Lord Sumption tells stage 4 cancer patient her life is 'less valuable', *The Guardian* 17 Jan 2021: https://www.theguardian.com/law/2021/jan/17/jonathan-sumption-cancer-patient-life-less-valuable-others?CMP=Share_AndroidApp_Other

The principle of equity is important in NHS organ allocation, with those in most urgent need given organs first. This is a question of *distributive justice.* Philosopher John Rawls, famous for his views on social justice, argues for the principle of equity. This means that in general we need to treat everyone fairly, but those who are most vulnerable and needy may also be in most need of scarce resources, as they are most likely to die without them. He argues that the people in greatest need, and those who are most severely ill and vulnerable, should be allocated organs first. Rawls' philosophy is often used to defend the right to equal access to health care. He stated that '*each person possesses an inviolability founded on justice that even the welfare of society as a whole cannot override*'.[53] Many religious thinkers agree with this, basing their beliefs on the Sanctity of Life principle. The Qur'an says '*be good to parents, and relatives, and orphans, and the needy*' (2:83). The idea that everyone is made in God's image means many traditional religious thinkers are very concerned about judging some organ recipients to be more worthy than others.

The allocation of resources is an important matter of judgement, the fourth principle of biomedical ethics, issue for American ethicists Beauchamp and Childress. How should we choose who to treat: should it be equal, or should people receive things on the basis of effort, contribution, or merit? Utilitarians and many ethicists disagree with Rawls and the Sanctity of Life, saying that we should distribute resources using a process like QALYs, which gives according to the amount of good it will do rather than the amount that someone needs it. This makes the best use of the organs that we have available and can save more lives.

Should some lifestyles stop people getting organs?
Some thinkers argue that people should not be given organs if their transplant needs are related to their own poor life choices, for example if someone has liver failure due to persistent alcoholism or smoking.

---

[53] John Rawls, *A Theory of Justice* (Harvard University Press, 1971), 3.

Doward and Campbell claim that a quarter of liver transplants are given to alcoholics. This seems to be unjust when there are many who have not abused their livers who are also waiting for transplants. It also seems to go against Utilitarian principles, as people who have previously abused their organs may do the same again.[54]

A famous UK example of this issue is Manchester United footballer George Best. In 2002, he was given a liver transplant due to liver cirrhosis brought on by his alcoholism. Best later resumed his alcohol consumption and died three years later.

There are many potential reasons for not putting an alcoholic on the organ donor list, which do not necessarily relate to discrimination. Continued alcoholism could mean the patient is unlikely to treat their new liver well, and may suffer from the same problems in the near future and need another transplant (*point 2*). Also, alcoholism can be connected with non-adherence to taking immunosuppressants (*point 4*). This means that people who are alcoholic may not take the medication they need in order for the transplant to be a success.

Giving organs to those who may go on to abuse them may also not be cost-effective. Those in poorer areas are more likely to smoke, drink and

---

[54] Jamie Doward and Denis Campbell, *Transplant row over organs for drinkers,* The Guardian, 15 Feb 2009: Transplant row over organs for drinkers | Organ donation | The Guardian .

abuse drugs and *'these lifestyle choices contribute to the need for medical intervention'*. People with poor lifestyles are costing the taxpayer more money.[55]

On the other hand, many people who have 'bad' lifestyle choices may not have been given adequate education or received equal chances in life in the first place. Likewise, if restrictions on treatment are going to be imposed, shouldn't these also be put in place for people who undertake risky activities such as skiing and skydiving? And where would we draw the line on deciding who lived a good life, or whose life was more valuable? Couldn't this lead to a slippery slope of only allocating organs to people of a certain demographic or profession? Refusing to allocate organs on the basis of lifestyle could also go against one of the basic principles of the NHS, which states that it *'meets the needs of everyone'* and that it is *'based on clinical need, not ability to pay'*. Many deontologists and religious ethicists would say that this fails to treat people with dignity.

In 2010, Michael Selkirk, a long-term alcoholic in Ontario, Canada, suffered from acute liver failure. He was denied a transplant on the grounds that he needed to be sober for six months before he would be added to the list of potential recipients. He died after two weeks. His wife, Debra Selkirk, issued a constitutional challenge to this decision, on the grounds that her husband was denied his universal right to health care. Philosopher Arthur Schafer argues that doctors should not be making moral decisions for patients: *'Doctors aren't priests, ministers*

---

[55] For more on whether George Best should have received an organ transplant, see Simone Bedford and Elaine Jones, 'Should lifestyle choices affect access to a transplant?', *Nursing Times*, 18 July 2014: https://www.nursingtimes.net/clinical-archive/public-health-clinical-archive/should-lifestyle-choices-affect-access-to-transplant-18-07-2014/

and rabbis, and they're not moral judges'.[56] He argues that a transplant is worthwhile if it will give the patient any extension to their life, even if this may not be as long as someone else's. In a similar case in Montreal in August 2022, 44-year-old Daljinder Nahar was denied a liver transplant due to his alcoholism even though his family members offered to donate parts of their livers as living donors. He died a few days later. His family argued that the refusal to contemplate giving him a donation, even from one of them, was discrimination against him due to his alcohol problem.[57]

---

[56] See Aleksandra Sagan, 'Organ donation ethics: How doctors decide who gets a transplant', *CBC News*, 29 Jan 2015: https://www.cbc.ca/news/health/organ-donation-ethics-how-doctors-decide-who-gets-a-transplant-1.2936439

[57] See Antoni Nerestant, 'Dying man's family pushing for liver transplant say Quebec's rules are unfair', *CBC News*, 11 August 2022: https://www.cbc.ca/news/canada/montreal/liver-transplant-much-chum-life-refusal-1.6545791

RELIGIOUS VIEWS

A Christian view

The Bible encourages people to support the poor and needy. There are many examples of Jesus helping the disadvantaged in society. He told his disciples: *'Heal the sick, raise the dead, cleanse those who have leprosy, drive out demons. Freely you have received; freely give'*. (Matthew 10:8). This suggests that healing (whether that is through miracles or medicine) is a positive thing and life and health should be good aims for Christians. Most Christians also argue that it is highly discriminatory to refuse to treat someone on the grounds of age, illness, or disability, and note that Jesus chose to spend time with vulnerable and marginalised people. Due to their focus on the Sanctity of Life, many Christians are strongly in favour of the principle of equity in organ allocation.

However, as Meilaender notes, staying alive is not always the main aim in a faith that believes strongly in an afterlife free from pain. While in most cases trying to preserve life is a high moral good, many Christians acknowledge that the choice not to participate in further treatment such as receiving a new organ can be equally valid.

NON-RELIGIOUS VIEWS

Paul Menzel

American philosopher Paul Menzel follows a broadly deontological view on this topic, arguing that organs should be allocated on the basis of equity rather than utility.

Menzel notes that if someone is at immediate risk of death, we should prioritise doing what it takes to rescue them, whatever the financial cost. He says *'The actual actions that people take provide ample evidence that we will expend great effort and large resources to avert death'.*[58]

There is ample evidence to support Menzel's theory. In Copiapo, Chile, in 2010, 33 miners became trapped 700 metres underground after a mine shaft collapsed. Their plight captured the world's attention. The subsequent rescue effort took two months and cost USD $20 million. It involved three drilling rig teams, most Chilean government ministries, NASA, and twelve different international corporations. A new capsule was invented and built to rescue the miners. They were all saved. However, mining accidents in Chile are common, with an average of 34 people dying each year in such events since 2000. So was over $600,000 per person too much to pay for the lives of these men, when the same amount could have been spent trying to reform mining safety practices and potentially saving more lives? Menzel argues that as humans we instinctively want to save people in dire straits and a cost-benefit analysis goes against our common humanity. In the same way, allocating organs to people who need them most desperately is simply a human thing to do.

Menzel says that this also applies to those with disabilities: *'few among us... honestly believe that it is less important for society to save the lives of persons with paraplegia than the lives of others to full health. The equal value of life-saving regardless of final health state appears to dominate'.* He emphasises that having hope and the potential of being treated is really important, and many people think maintaining equality is important too. Many people *'consider it inequitable to exclude some from treatment that most others receive'.* To preserve both autonomy and utility, perhaps we need to think of allocation beyond QALYs and other Utilitarian calculations and consider people more as individuals.[59]

---

[58] Menzel, Paul, 'The Allocation of Scarce Resources', in *Blackwell Guide to Medical Ethics*, eds. Rosamund Rhodes, Leslie P. Francis, Anita Silvers (2007), 305-322, 314.

[59] Menzel, 'The Allocation of Scarce Resources', 317.

QALYs

As we have seen, the utilitarian measure of QALYs is at the opposite end of the scale to Menzel's equity-based thought. Following the logic of QALYs, people qualify for organ transplants on the basis of their likely outcome.

Ultimately, we can see all of these thinkers' views on a scale of equity-utility.

TASK

Where would you place your own view on this scale?

Allocate according to need — Arthur Schaefer — John Rawls — Paul Menzel — Many Christians — Doward & Campbell — QALYs — Allocate according to utility

DISCUSSION TASK: WHO GETS THE HEART?

Let's imagine five different people: Max, Jasmine, Ellie, Shapi and Teddy. They all have heart failure and urgently need a new heart in order to survive. A heart becomes available, and they are all a matching blood type. They became in need of a transplant in the order they are shown in the image, with Max waiting the longest.

Max is 70 and also has diabetes. He has had heart failure for years but it is getting worse.

Shapi is 25 and unemployed. She has bipolar disorder. Her heart failure is the result of an overdose of medication.

Ellie is 38 and works in administration. She had an unidentified heart defect leading to heart failure.

Jasmine is 45 and works in medical research. She helped to develop the Covid vaccine and won an award for her life-saving developments. She was in a car accident, which has led to heart failure.

Teddy is 41 and has recently lost his job in construction due to his alcoholism. He also urgently needs a liver transplant.

Who do you think should receive the heart?

Ideally, all five of these patients should receive transplants. However, in practice, Max, Shapi and Teddy could all be excluded from the donor list, as Max has medical comorbidity (*point 5*), Shapi has psychiatric comorbidity (*point 6*), and Teddy has a history of alcohol abuse (*point 2*) and the need for multiple transplants (*point 10*). We could also question whether Max and Shapi will have good quality of life (*point 9*) after the transplant, and we could question whether Shapi might be at risk of non-adherence (*point 4*) due to her psychiatric issues.

If the process was fully equitable, each of these patients would have an equal chance of receiving a heart. Assuming all of these patients were placed on the transplant list, Max would receive the heart if he had been waiting the longest.

If the process was based on QALYs, Max would be excluded almost immediately due to his age and other health condition. He may not live for many more years. Shapi would be unlikely to be allocated high QALYs due to her other issues, although theoretically she could live the longest. In this case, Ellie would be most likely to receive the heart as she would be most likely to have the most years in good health. It would be difficult to decide QALYs for Teddy, as it is impossible to predict whether he will be able to overcome his alcohol abuse in the future.

If the process was based on some other system such as 'social merit', Jasmine might be given the heart due to perceived services to the community. Shapi and Teddy would be unlikely ever to receive a donor heart. Many critics of a social merit system, including those who believe in the Sanctity of Life, argue that this is an unhelpful form of ableism and would lead to a slippery slope in which only supposedly 'good' people who meet certain criteria were able to access vital services.

8 END OF LIFE

Every life ends in death, but today death is very medicalised, with 50% of people in the UK dying in hospitals even though 70% would prefer to die at home. However, what exactly constitutes death is not always certain: brain death means irretrievable loss of brain function, whereas circulatory death means the heart and lungs have stopped pumping oxygenated blood around the body. Both together mean certain death. But there are grey areas, such as life support, where a person's heart is kept going artificially, and a vegetative state, where brain function appears to be minimal, where it is impossible to tell whether someone will come back to a state of conscious life. In terms of treatment around the time of death, medical care aims to prolong life and delay death through giving further treatment, whereas social care aims to ensure that death is as comfortable as possible and that a person's holistic needs are met. Assisted dying includes both assisted suicide, where an individual is helped to end their life, and euthanasia, where a patient's life is ended at their request by medical professionals.

On 15 April 1989, during an FA Cup semi-final between Liverpool and Nottingham Forest a tragedy occurred that would set off a series of events that significantly shifted not only how we understand death, but the value of life as well.

During the game, a failure of police crowd control led to crush behind the Liverpool goal. A crush had formed at the outer gates, so Liverpool fans were let in through a side gate. However, police officers and club stewards failed to close the access tunnels first so thousands of fans were sent into already crowded standing pens. These failures led to the deaths of 94 people on that day, and a 95th victim in hospital a few days later. This infamous event is now known as the Hillsborough disaster.

Amongst the fans was 18-year-old, Tony Bland. He was not counted as one of the initial victims of the disaster, as although he survived the crush, he suffered severe brain damage that left him in a persistent vegetative state. After four years, as there had been no sign of improvement in his condition, the hospital – with the support of his parents – applied for a court order allowing him to 'die with dignity'. As a result, he became the first patient in English legal history to be allowed to die through the withdrawal of life-prolonging treatment (in this case his feeding tubes). He became known as the 96th Hillsborough disaster victim.

At an inquest into the disaster, his parents said their son lost his life four years before the court ruled he could die.

If we were to conduct a poll in class, the majority would undoubtably vote that killing for advantage or convenience is immoral. When pushed for reason, they might say to do so violates that person's 'right to life'. But things get a lot less clear cut when a person keeps asking to be killed, or is in never-ending pain, or is very dependent on others for care, or is a huge drain on finance or resources, or is 'living' in a state of permanent unconscious. Many in that same class would then sympathise with the person who feels permitted to end that person's life.

Most people, for instance, would have agreed with or at least understood the hope of Bland's family and his medical care teams that he would die sooner rather than later. Despite the media coverage about 'switching life support off', there was no such machine. He was receiving tube-feeding and ordinary nursing care – as are many people in the UK today. But he was unlikely ever to regain consciousness and was a significant burden on others. The question was: was he even still alive?

Sanctity of life vs Quality of Life

Before medical advances definitions of death were fairly straightforward – it was simply a lack of breath or a lack of heartbeat for a sustained period of time. We're now capable of maintaining those aspects of life and have a host of ways of detecting brain activity and consciousness. So what does the 'end of life' actually mean?

Peter Singer has argued that there has been a shift in Western liberal societies where traditional sanctity of life arguments are giving way to a new liberal quality of life argument. In the case of Tony Bland, we apparently saw a decision that seems to deny the sanctity of life principle: however, it is interesting to explore the thinking behind it.

The judges in Tony Bland's case explored the concept of whether he really was a living human being because of his lack of consciousness. This implies that only human beings with certain qualifications are entitled to the respect or value given through the sanctity of life principle. Specifically, the value of life is based on an individual's capacity for mental activity and consciousness. When those things are gone, then life is gone.

There was also the consideration that Tony Bland's continued life was a source of indignity and humiliation to him, and that to be living in such a way is no life at all.

However, Lord Mustill, who ultimately approved the decision to discontinue Bland's tube-feeding, confessed the hollowness of the claim that this was in Bland's 'best interests.' He suggested that the interests of the family, the medical staff, and the paying community were decisive here. He concluded that *'the distressing truth which must not be shirked is that the proposed conduct is not in the best interests of Tony Bland'.* In short, he suggested that the value of his life was compromised to serve the interests of others.

Whether we take the position that the value of life can be lost, or whether it can be negated by another value, is clearly inconsistent with the traditional doctrine of the sanctity of life. It creates a hierarchy in which some people or types of life are assessed negatively, and thus can either be killed or 'allowed to die.' However, it is worth nothing that 'quality of life' judgements are incredibly subjective – it becomes a matter of personal choice, dictated by individual circumstance. Who then is to decide when life has ended?

DISCUSSION POINTS

Discuss the merits of the following opinions:

1. Legal Judges

2. Governments

3. Philosophers

4. Religious Leaders

5. Doctors

6. Individuals

9 END OF LIFE CARE

End of life care refers to the support given to people who in the last weeks, months or even years of their life. End of life care should help people to live as well as possible until the point of death, and to then die with dignity. It should take wishes and preferences into account but remain within the constraints of the law. End of life care can be further subdivided into two sections: medical and social care.

Medical care is typically thought of as the improvement of health through cure of disease, illness or injury. This can continue up until the end of life through attempts to delay death. Of course, a cure is not always possible, but there are often ongoing medical treatment options that can delay death.

Social care recognises that patient care needs to be holistic in its approach; this can involve the use of medication to alleviate pain but also seeks to enhance a person's life through psychological, social and spiritual support. This could be for both the patient and their family.

In Scotland, around 63,000 deaths are recorded each year. The most common causes of death in Scotland are cancer, diseases of the circulatory system (like heart disease or strokes), diseases of the digestive system, and external causes of morbidity and mortality, a broad umbrella term which covers things like drug related death as well as obesity.

According to official statistics in Scotland, since March 2020, 26,730 people have died at home or outside a hospital or care setting, an increase of 7,826 on the five-year average. Whilst more people claim that they would prefer to die at home, research by end-of-life charity Marie Curie has found that up to three quarters of carers looking after someone with a terminal illness at home struggled to get the care and support they needed.

Hospice care

One form of social care is in the provision of hospice care, which aims to improve the lives of people with an incurable illness or disease. It aims to provide support from the point of diagnosis to life's end. Care may not be continuous but can be accessed as the patient requires it. Hospice care places a high value on autonomy and aims to maintain the dignity, respect and wishes of the patient. Holistic in nature, it looks beyond medical care to consider the emotional, social, practical, and spiritual needs of the patience, their family and carers. Whilst much hospice care occurs within 'in-patient units', they also provide help and support to people in their own homes. Many hospices also drive education and research, aiming to provide the best care possible.

Hospice Care in Edinburgh and the Lothians is provided by St. Columba's Hospice. It costs £10.7 million a year to run, 25% of which comes from the NHS and the other 75% is provided through public donation. Whilst this is an incredible amount of money to find each year, their independence allows them to quickly adapt to the needs of the community. However, St. Columba's estimate that there are 11,000 people who could benefit from Hospice Care who they are currently unable to help.

Hospital Care

Both medical and social care can be provided within a hospital setting. Doctors, nurses, and other healthcare professionals work together to cure illnesses, but when this is not possible, many hospitals have specialist palliative care teams to care for people who are nearing the end of life.

These specialist palliative care teams provide advice on pain and symptom control, and can also help with transfer to a hospice or other care facility to fit with individual needs.

In the UK, it is legal to ask for treatment to be withdrawn at any time stopping medical care or life-sustaining treatment, and to allow death to take its course. 'No not resuscitate' orders, known as 'DNRs', mean that doctors do not have to try to resuscitate someone if they stop breathing or go into cardiac arrest. This allows for a level of autonomy within end-of-life care, provided the patient is thought to be making informed decisions with the absence of coercion.

For those who are worried about diminishing capacity, they are also able to appoint someone else to make decisions for them or they can state in writing the type of treatment they would like to receive in the future. In Scotland, this is known as a an 'advance directive' (commonly referred to as a 'living will') and is a document which expresses the wishes of an individual as to their treatment should they become mentally incapacitated and unable to make decisions in the future.

MORAL ISSUES

Is it the role of Government to provide end of life care?

Public and institutional policies guide medical treatment decisions near the end of life in multiple ways. They may, for example, determine what treatment options are lawful and unlawful, who may provide various treatments, and what resources are available to pay for different treatment options.

In 2010, a Bill was introduced to the Scottish Parliament to require *'palliative care to be provided to persons with a life-limited condition and to members of such person's families'*. This was ultimately withdrawn on the basis that current legislation was reasonably robust and there had not been adequate time to see if the changes the Government had made would improve care.

In 2014 the World Health Assembly – the governing body of the World Health Organisation – passed a resolution requiring all governments to recognise palliative care and to make provision for it in their national health policies. In response to that, the Scottish Government published a *Strategic Framework for Action on Palliative and End of Life Care*. This set out a commitment that the Government would work to ensure that by 2021 everyone in Scotland who needed palliative care would have access to it.

However, more recently in March 2023, hospice leaders met with the Scottish Government ministers to warn of a *'looming palliate care crisis'* pointing to a short fall in hospice funding. Although Palliative Care is now a statuary requirement, hospices require charitable donations for the majority of their income. There is a fear that rising costs will force some hospices to close, and access to patient care will be even more restricted. The First Minister has committed to ensuring *'conversations take place about the pressures hospices are facing... and to see what support [they] might be able to provide.'*[60]

Who should have the authority to make treatment decisions?

Patient autonomy is often at the heart of end-of-life care, working on the principles that everyone has the right to do whatever they want to do for themselves without violations of rules and regulations. Sometimes in end-of-life care, patients don't want to continue their treatments but what should happen if they or those who speak for them do want to continue treatment, but doctors do not believe it to be in the patient's best interest?

Such a conflict was found in the case of Charlie Gard in 2017, Charlie was born with an exceptionally rare genetic condition called encephalomyopathic mitochondrial DNA depletion syndrome (MDDS). Although he appeared perfectly healthy when he was born, his health soon began to deteriorate, and Great Ormond Street Hospital (GOSH) said his prognosis was bleak. Eventually, Charlie was unable to breath unaided, could not open his eyes, move his arms or legs and had severe brain damage. Many of his organs were also affected and the doctors could not be certain whether he felt pain.

---

[60] See Frankie McPherson, 'Hospice chiefs: Let's discuss fair funding', *HealthandCare.Scot*, 27 March 2023: https://healthandcare.scot/stories/3420/hospices-funding-government-support

His parents wanted to take Charlie to America for an experimental treatment, after the US President Donald Trump tweeted support. American doctors co-signed a letter which suggested data form an unpublished study showed a therapy that 'might' help but that there was no time for a trial. As no human or animal had ever been undergone this treatment, GOSH pursued a different option. By the time this was approved, Charlie's condition had worsened. The doctors decided that the most humane approach was to allow Charlie to 'die with dignity', which aligns with the UK legal position that a patient cannot demand a treatment that is not in their best interests and that doctors need not strive to preserve life at all costs. Charlie's parents disagreed and took the Hospital to court, however ultimately the High Court agreed with the hospital, as did the Supreme Court and the European Court, and treatment was withdrawn.[61]

The doctrine of double effect (DDE)

Opioids and sedatives provide effective relief for the frequently distressing symptoms of pain, shortness of breath and agitation as the end of life approaches. The frequent misconception among professionals is that the life of the patient may be shortened by increasing doses of these drugs – a belief often shared by patients and their families. The doctrine of double effect provides justification for such a consequence but raises concerns that it may protect dangerous practice.

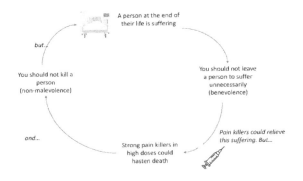

---

[61] See Nick Triggle, 'Charlie Gard: a case that changed everything?', *BBC News*, 29 July 2017: https://www.bbc.co.uk/news/health-40644896

The DDE states that an action (such as an increase in opioid dose) that the professional foresees may shorten life – but does not intend to have that result – is justified provided that the intention is to benefit the patient and not shorten their life. For example, if a patient was in so much pain that the 'normal' dose of pain killer is ineffectual, a higher does may be given if doctor believes this may shorten life.

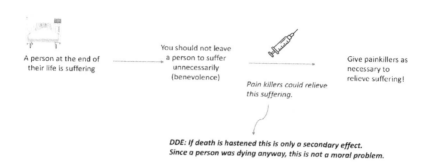

A person at the end of their life is suffering — You should not leave a person to suffer unnecessarily (benevolence) — Give painkillers as necessary to relieve suffering!

Pain killers could relieve this suffering.

DDE: If death is hastened this is only a secondary effect. Since a person was dying anyway, this is not a moral problem.

There is a fear that the DDE may just be used to disguise an intentional shortening of life. However, even when opioids and sedatives are used in line with accepted palliative care practice there is no credible research to show that they shorten life.

In his book *Causing Death and Saving Lives*, British Philosopher Jonathan Glover argues that continued treatment and medical intervention at the point where death is inevitably approaching is simply *'prolonging the act of dying'*, is expensive and serves little purpose. With this ruled out, three alternatives would remain: a neutral stance neither slowing nor prolonging dying, 'double effect' giving medication that will relieve pain but could also speed up death, or intentional killing. Glover argues that the neutral policy will hurt friends and family: *'the distress a lingering death causes to their family will normally be a reason for thinking an accelerated death desirable'* but that *'it may be unpleasant for doctors and nurses to take part in a positive act which will speed up death'*. He also describes double effect doctrine as an *'intellectually dubious rigmarole: saying that one consequence is intended while the other is not'*. However, he sees this policy of giving pain relief that may speed up death as normally the most reasonable, as it has the aim of relieving pain. He argues that at times the 'unintended by-product' of speeding up death could at times be seen as a positive thing, and at least saves us from the 'emotional revulsion' that could be caused by intentional killing. In summary, Glover disagrees with the DDE, but agrees with its practical outcome.[62]

It is important to note the difference between DDE and assisting dying or active euthanasia: assisted dying occurs by a patient's choice and could dramatically shorten their life by months or years, whereas DDE is only applied in the final stages of death as a means of decreasing pain in a person's final moments.

What constitutes care?
Hydration and nutrition are obviously thought of a necessary for survival, so it seems counterintuitive in many ways to consider 'care' as withdrawing these things. However, when they become 'clinically assisted' they are viewed as a treatment rather than case. Therefore, when they are deemed to no longer offer benefit, they can be withdrawn on the basis that the harm of continuing them outweigh any benefit. However, as with the DDE the patient is not deemed to be dying from a lack of hydration or nutrition, but rather they are dying and therefore do not require these things.

Can there be value in suffering?
When considering end of life care, we often conflate pain with suffering. However, the two are not the same. Not everyone who is suffering is in physical pain. For example, a patient may believe that a loss of bodily control constitutes unbearable suffering at the moment that they must rely on others for their needs.

However, particularly for those from a faith perspective some argue that the end of life provides a final opportunity to develop – to accept

---

[62] Jonathan Glover, *Causing death and saving lives* (Penguin, 1990), 114.

deterioration, to realise the co-dependency we all have, and that for many – a faith that there will be life on the other side of death.

There is also the opportunity for the community around them to show that 'suffering' can be lessened through support and care.

RELIGIOUS RESPONSES

Church of Scotland
In response to the 2010 Bill brought to the Scottish Parliament to require *'palliative care to be provided to persons with a life-limited condition and to members of such person's families'*, the Church of Scotland and Salvation Army issued a joint response.

They argued that *'all members of the Church are called to share Christ's love and compassion; to care for and support those facing death. Incapacitating illness should not be trivialised, yet God made us for relationship, both with Him and in supporting communities which value all their members.'* However, they also acknowledged that *'People fear not only pain but indignity and becoming a burden to their loved ones. Caring for the dying can be a relentless and often painfully heavy experience.'*[63]

They reaffirmed the church's position that human life is sacred and that as a result we have a duty to not allow people to suffer alone. They pointed to the great work done by the hospices, and organisations such as Marie Curie Cancer Care, Macmillan Cancer Support, and the Maggie's Centres who also rely upon charitable giving. But they highlighted that these facilities are provided for cancer sufferers only, and there are a great many people dying in Scotland from other

---

[63] Alan Dixon & Ian Galloway, 'Official Response to Proposed Palliative Care (Scotland) Bill', Church of Scotland, 1 September 2010: https://churchofscotland.org.uk/__data/assets/pdf_file/0015/4227/palliative_c are_response_sep2010.pdf

illnesses, such as heart failure or simply old age. They also highlighted the inequality of access to care for people living in rural areas maintaining that all lives should be viewed as equal. They concluded that that greater priority must be given to improving palliative care not just in care homes, hospitals, and hospices but also for the sick in their own homes.

Roman Catholic Church

The Sanctity of Life principle rests at the heart of Roman Catholic doctrine, and maintains that all human life has value as a result of their unique relationship with God. In many cases, this is taken to mean that life should be protected at all cost, however in practice, particularly in relation to the end of life, there has been a division of opinion.

In response to the Charlie Gard case – the young baby with encephalomyopathic mitochondrial DNA depletion syndrome – the Pontifical Academy for Life wrote that whilst life is a gift, 'we must also accept the limits of medicine and … avoid aggressive medical procedures that are disproportionate to any expected results or excessively burdensome to the patient or the family'.

Public opinion was generally against the hospital in this instance, in part because it was hard not to sympathise with the parents' distress, and Pope Francis issued a further message via the Vatican press office saying: 'The Holy Father follows with affection and emotion the case of little Charlie Gard and expresses his own closeness to his parents. For them he prays, hoping that their desire to accompany and care for their own child to the end is not ignored.'

However, the Catholic bishops of England and Wales then issued a statement maintaining that it was 'important to remember that all involved in these agonising decisions have sought to act with integrity and for Charlie's good as they see it'. Within the same week, the Anscombe Bioethics Centre, a Catholic institute based in the UK, criticised the hospital for eroding the parents' rights and arguing that as they have good intentions, they should have the power to decide on his treatment and care.

It can be seen that the Roman Catholic perspective, whilst maintaining the value of life, does not see that death must be put off at all costs. Equally, it allows for the withdrawal of treatment on the basis that any continued treatment would not significantly reverse or prevent the deterioration of life. This is seen as omission rather than an action to end life, and is also seen to uphold the idea that ultimately God both gives and takes away life. Finally, it allows the doctrine of double effect, on the ground that the aim is to relieve pain (in line with the beneficence, the second principle of Biomedical Ethics).

NON-RELIGIOUS RESPONSES

As previously noted, the World Health Assembly – the governing body of the World Health Organisation – requires all governments to recognise palliative care and to make provision for it in their national health policies. The Scottish Government, in recognition of this, published 'a palliative and end of life care strategic framework for action' and is still working with stakeholders to implement it.[64]

Human Rights
Human rights are a subject devolved to Scotland by the Scotland Act 1998. These civil and political rights are protected by the UK Human Rights Act 1998 (HRA) and provisions in the Scotland Act 1998. These rights come from the European Convention on Human Rights (ECHR). The UK Human Rights Act 1998 imposes an obligation to facilitate a 'good death' – in practice this means considering Rights such as the Right to Liberty, the Right to be free from inhuman and degrading treatment, the Right to freedom of thought, conscience and religion and the Right to private and family life, home and correspondence. The HRA places a legal duty on health services to uphold these standards, and demands that any laws must be compatible with these rights.

On paper, the Scottish Government is complying with the HRA through their commitment to providing palliative care. However, research by Marie Curie reveals that people in Scotland are still experiencing inequality when it comes to palliative end of life care. The Government has so far fallen short of their ambition to provide palliative care for those who need it. This inequity is exacerbated for those dying with non-cancer treatments, older people, and women. Scotland has an ageing population, meaning that by 2040 up to 10,000 more people could be dying each year with a need for palliative care.

Diversity in Healthcare
Helen Dempsey-Henofer, a clinical social worker, wrote an article in 2019 entitled 'Death without God: Non-religious Perspectives on End-of-Life Care'. Looking primarily at end-of-life care in the USA, she sought to

---

[64] For more information, see:
https://www.gov.scot/binaries/content/documents/govscot/publications/strate gy-plan/2015/12/strategic-framework-action-palliative-end-life-care/

highlight how underrepresented non-religious people are in end-of-life care research.[65]

She highlighted that the founder of the modern hospice movement – Dame Cicely Saunders – did so because of her Christian beliefs and a desire to find a new way to 'serve' others. The initial advice was that hospices providers should 'regard their work as a religious vocation.' Although many hospices – like St. Columba's in Edinburgh – site secular values as their guiding basis, they still have many links to the church through the provision of funding and of course, in their name.

Demsey-Henofer's research was supported through surveying non-religious people on social media groups using questionnaires and surveys. Whilst this means of research has limitations, it did reveal a general trend of dissatisfaction at the level of care provided for non-religious people. She highlighted that even something as generic as a chaplain visiting a non-religious person and saying 'I'll keep you in my prayers' can be discomforting to someone without faith. Whilst palliative care is meant to provide 'spiritual care', she concludes that much more consideration needs to be given to what this looks like for atheist patients.

DISCUSSION QUESTIONS

1. What tools can people use to decide when it's time to stop medical care? Is this a matter of right and wrong?
2. Is the doctrine of double effect just 'euthanasia by the back door'? Are believers in the Strong Sanctity of Life being hypocritical when they use DDE to justify end-of life pain relief?
3. Should we have a bigger focus on palliative care in our health system?

---

[65] Helen Dempsey-Henofer, 'Death without God: Nonreligious Perspectives on End-of-Life Care', *Diversity and Equality in Health and Care* (2019), 16/4: https://www.primescholars.com/articles/death-without-god-nonreligious-perspectives-on-endoflife-care-95005.html

TASK

American Ethicists Beauchamp and Childress stated that there are 4 Principles of Biomedical Ethics:

1. Autonomy: giving people the ability to make their own decisions
2. Benevolence: doing what is best for a person
3. Non-maleficence: 'do no harm'
4. Judgement: make balanced decisions for individuals[66]

How can we use all of these principles to make the best decisions about end-of-life care? Which do you think is most important? Which is least important? Why?

(note: you could also ask this question about any of the other chapters in this book)

---

[66] See Tom Beauchamp & James Childress, *Principles of Biomedical Ethics* (Oxford, 1979).

10 ASSISTED DYING

Assisted dying is where a person is given medical assistance to end their life. It can refer to 'assisted suicide' or various forms of euthanasia. Whilst the terms may often be conflated it is important to understand the differences between assisted suicide and euthanasia because the two concepts raise varying moral issues and are treated differently by legal systems beyond the UK.

Assisted suicide is the act of deliberating assisting another person to kill themselves. For example, by providing a person with the means to kill themselves but the action which directly causes death is performed by the one wishing to die. In contrast, active euthanasia involves specific actions that bring about death - such as a lethal injection. Whilst Switzerland may be well-known for its 'death tourism', in fact it only permits assisted suicide and has stopped short of allowing active euthanasia.

Whilst England and Wales decriminalised suicide in 1961, Scotland has made no move to decriminalise it. Equally, there is no specific crime of assisting a suicide in Scotland (in England it is punishable by up to 14 years in prison). But it is possible that helping a person to die could lead to prosecution for murder, culpable homicide or reckless endangerment. Active euthanasia is also illegal, but as we have seen in the end-of-life care unit it is legal to withdraw medical care and other life sustaining treatments. This would be referred to as 'passive euthanasia' as it is simply allowing the person to die from natural causes.

The latest attempt to change the law in Scotland has come from Liberal Democrat MSP Liam McArthur. He lodged a Bill in 2021 to enable competent adults who are terminally ill to be provided at their request with assistance to end their life. This contained certain caveats, such as that they must be diagnosed with a progressive disease which can reasonably be expected to cause their death, they must be 16 years of age of over, and a resident of Scotland for at least 12 months.[67]

There is considerable public support for legalisation of some form of assisted dying in the UK, with recent polls suggesting that 84% of the British public, and 80% of people who identify as religious, would like it to be legalised. Promoting autonomy and compassion for those who are suffering are generally cited as the two main reasons to legalise assisted dying. However, the majority of those who work in palliative care, and have the most experience with death as part of their day to day lives, remain opposed. They argue that it would be in danger of disproportionately affecting those who are the most vulnerable including people from minority groups and those living in poverty who were not able to access the social care they needed for a 'good' death.

MORAL ISSUES

A slippery slope?
Euthanasia in the Netherlands is regulated by the 'Termination of Life on Request and Assisted Suicide (Review Procedures) Act' which was passed in 2001 and took effect in 2002. It states that euthanasia and assisted suicide are not punishable if the doctor acts in accordance with certain criteria including:

- The patient must request it.
- The patient's suffering must be unbearable and hopeless.
- The patient must be fully informed.
- There must be an absence of reasonable alternatives.

---

[67] For more on this proposal, see: https://www.parliament.scot/bills-and-laws/proposals-for-bills/proposed-assisted-dying-for-terminally-ill-adults-scotland-bill

- Another doctor must agree.
- The doctor must follow an agreed method.

Patients do not need to be suffering from a specific disease of have a certain diagnosis, and mental illness is included as a reason for 'unbearable and hopeless' suffering. For example, in 2016 an otherwise healthy woman was granted euthanasia on the basis of 'prolonged grief disorder' following her husband's death 12 months before.

However, there have been changes to the code of practice since the law has been introduced. For example, since 2020 doctors have been able to 'slip a sedative' into the food or drink of patients with severe dementia if there is a concern they will become 'disturbed, agitated or aggressive' – provided the patient had previously given written consent. The country also expanded the law to include children between the ages of one and 12 with parental consent. The law already allowed non-voluntary euthanasia for babies who haven't yet reached their first birthday.

Critics of euthanasia point to the expanding laws in the Netherlands of evidence of the 'slippery slope' effect. This theory asserts that a relatively small first step leads to a chain of events culminating in a significant effect. With reference to the assisted dying debate, the slippery slope argument claims that acceptance for assisted dying will invariably lead to the acceptance of practices that are currently deemed unacceptable, such as non-voluntary euthanasia.

A common counterargument is to say that this is fearmongering and that it is still possible to draw a line. For example, just because we have a law that allows adults to drink alcohol, we'll never allow children to do so. However, the law in the Netherlands has gradually changed; whilst it first allowed euthanasia for terminal illness it now has a far greater scope. If, these things – like euthanasia for children – had been examined first, would they have been permitted?

Does denying assisted dying violate autonomy?

Arguments for assisted dying frequently refer to the right to self-determination or autonomy and free will. We expect to have control over our bodies in matters of life, and many argue we should have the same control in matters of death. Advocates of assisted dying argue that it should be an option for a competent adult, who is able to decide, and ultimately able to bring about their own death.

However, pitted against this is the question of whether self-determination is genuinely possible when choosing your own death. The vast majority of decisions that we make are in relation to other people. Our decisions are affected by other people, and equally our decisions affect others. This is particularly the case in assisted dying when a person's autonomy requires others to approve of, if not participate in, the deliberate act of taking of their life. A person's death and the manner of their death is not an isolated event. These things have consequences, not least in the bereavement experience of those who are left behind, and the moral responsibility they may feel they carry in having been approving or complicit in a suicide. Additionally, one must consider whether the decision itself can be autonomous – imagine a situation in which an old person chooses to die because they feel as they are a burden to their children or relatives – that decision is arguably more about other people rather than autonomous value. Some may even argue that a person would only view themselves as a burden because society has demanded that we view dependency as a negative.

Any chance in legislation also needs to consider what is right for all – even if personal rights are restricted in some way. Currently, one is not 'free' to do all kinds of things because to allow it would be failing to protect others. For example, I am not free to drive beyond the speed limit, because I would be putting others in danger. Critics of assisted suicide point out that to allow it, whilst it would grant people autonomy, it could also allow for coercion even subliminally, perhaps implying that those who are a burden should do the 'right thing' and choose death to avoid inconveniencing others. Another point is whether we as individuals actually ever truly know what's best for ourselves.

Who should assist in dying?
In Switzerland, whilst a doctor provides the prescription for lethal substances, they are not required to administer them or to be there when they are taken. The vast majority of assisted suicides are supervised by members of 'Dignitas': a non-profit society who advocate for choice in relation to end-of-life care.

Canada operates a very different system, known as 'MAID' or Medical Assistance in Dying. Since 2016, both euthanasia and assisted suicide have been legal for people over the age of 18 and who meet certain conditions, such as having a serious condition, disease or disability that causes unbearable suffering with a reasonably foreseeable death. In 2023, Canda's Parliament decided not to extend this to people suffering from mental health conditions for at least another year, but as it stands, euthanasia is now the leading cause of death in Canada.

Unlike Switzerland, where suicide is witnessed by non-medical volunteers, MAID can be provided by physicians and nurse practitioners. Others including pharmacists, family members, friends, or health care providers can also help in its provision. In an interview with the BBC, one Canadian doctor – Dr Madeline Li – recalled the first time she helped a patient die: *'It was like stepping off a cliff, that first one'*, Dr Li said. *'Then time passes and it normalises'*.[68]

---

[68] See Holly Honderich, 'Who can die? Canada wrestles with euthanasia for the mentally ill', BBC News, 14 January 2023: https://www.bbc.co.uk/news/world-us-canada-64004329

In the UK, to be registered with the General Medical Council, a doctor agrees *'make the care of the patient their first concern.'* Can care constitute killing? And if so, should a doctor play an active role in death?

In 2020, the British Medical Journal conducted a survey of their members on doctor-assisted suicide. They found that whilst 50% of doctors would personally support a law to allow doctors to prescribe lethal drugs to patients for the purpose of suicide, only 36% would participate in the process to prescribe them. In relation to active euthanasia, 37% would support a law to allow doctors to administer the drugs to end a person's life, but only 26% would participate in the process. Overall, medical students were generally more supportive, and GPs generally more opposed, than most other branches of practice. These specialties tended to be generally more supportive: anaesthetics, emergency medicine, intensive care, and obstetrics and gynaecology. Whereas these specialties tended to be generally more opposed: clinical oncology, general practice, geriatric medicine, and palliative care. The survey did not explore what specifically caused the difference of opinion but did show a trend that the majority would not want to participate in assisted dying.[69]

In the aforementioned interview, Dr Li stressed repeatedly that a physician's personal opinions should not influence how they assess a patient for assisted death. But she has significant concerns about Canada's program, arguing that *'Making death too ready a solution disadvantages the most vulnerable people, and actually lets society off the hook. I don't think death should be society's solution for its own failures'.*

Does assisted dying violate the sanctity of life?
Whilst the majority of moral debate remains relatively civilised, there are some issues in today's world that have the power to become incredibly heated – undoubtably including the termination of pregnancy, capital punishment, and of course, assisted dying.

---

[69] For more information on this survey and the BMA's stance on assisted dying, see: https://www.bma.org.uk/advice-and-support/ethics/end-of-life/physician-assisted-dying/physician-assisted-dying-survey

For many, there seems to be some visceral reaction to the deliberate termination of another human being – even for those in favour, it is not a decision made lightly. This leads to the question of whether this life is 'sacrosanct' in some way i.e., the concept that life is too important or valuable to be terminated, even if that life is deemed to be insufferable.

However, it is interesting to explore what exactly makes life sacred. Traditionally, the 'sanctity of life' has been deemed to be a religious construct: as life is God given, it follows that it is sacred. But the sanctity of life has equally appeared in non-religious philosophy as well, such as the writings of Immanuel Kant who contended that 'moral law' is derived from our powers of reason from the 'good will.' And that whilst this good will cannot be proved, if humans are deemed to have reason, they must have equal moral consideration. Kant argued that rational human beings should be treated as an end in themselves and not as a means to something else. Our inherent value doesn't depend on anything else: it doesn't depend on whether we are having a good life that we enjoy, or whether we are making other people's lives better. We exist, so we have value.

The question is, can this innate value ever be lost? For Kant, only those capable of reason have worth – so could a dementia patient or someone in a coma have a life of value? And of course, if a person is suffering beyond measure, believes that they have lost their autonomy, or their dignity, is their life still sacred?

RELIGIOUS RESPONSES

Church of Scotland
Scottish theologian Professor John Swinton argues against assisted dying for several reasons.

Before his ordination in the Church of Scotland, Professor Swinton worked as a registered nurse specialising in psychiatry and learning disabilities. He worked for a number of years as a hospital chaplain, latterly as a community mental health chaplain before moving into the world of academia – founding the University of Aberdeen's Centre for Spirituality, Health and Disability.

Through his experience in these roles, he found that some of the reasons raised by euthanasia proponents are 'projection'. He argues that in relation to assisted dying, quite a lot of people use their imagination and project onto individuals what they think it would be like to have that experience and to use that as a rationale for a kind of ethical argument. For example, a person could imagine life as a paraplegic to be unbearable; they would be imagining losing their current situation and moving to a life of brokenness. However, Swinton highlights that with proper care this feeling need not be reality.[70]

He highlights that many people seeking assisted dying do so because they don't want to be a burden, because they cannot see a purpose to their life and often because they are lonely. When given a change to explore these feelings and to be part of a community, the same people stopped asking for death. Swinton highlights that assisted dying should never be an option put in place as a substitute for proper end-of-life care.

He admits that Christians view human life as inherently valuable because God places value on it – and this is not a belief shared by many in society. But he also highlights society tends to think the only thing that is valuable is choice – to live a life that is autonomous. However, ultimately this is a social construct and one that has only really taken hold in Western society. He points to the African philosophy of *ubuntu* – a concept in which your sense of self is shaped by your relationships with other people. Rather than focusing on the concept of 'I am', it is a way of living that begins with 'we are'. Applying this to end-of-life choices, it moves the debate away from the premise that certain lives (i.e., those with disabilities or illnesses) have less value and ensures that legislation is based on a wider societal perspective.

Professor Swinton's viewpoint was echoed by the Church of Scotland General Assembly, and they have stood against each of the Bills brought to the Scottish Government proposing the legalisation of assisted suicide. In 2003, they issued a report to reaffirm the Church's position which said they:

---

[70] See Julie Arliss & John Swinton, *Assisted Dying*, University of Aberdeen video (n.d.): https://www.abdn.ac.uk/sdhp/divinity-religious-studies/assisted-dying-1775.php

'Continue[s] to oppose any change to the legal position with regard to assisted suicide because of concerns about the effect any such change would have on the way society views its weakest and most vulnerable members, whilst recognising that many individuals and families face difficult decisions at the end of life, and urge the provision of better resources for palliative care.'[71]

Orthodox Judaism

As with the other monotheistic religions, Judaism teaches that life is sacred on the basis that it belongs to God. As he is the Creator, only he should decide when it begins or ends. Therefore, Orthodox Jews believe that is it wrong to hasten death in any way, and even the last moments are of value. According to traditional Jewish law, a terminally ill patient, defined as someone who is expected to die within 72 hours, is still considered a human being in all respects. As Baron Jakobovits, the former UK Chief Rabbi wrote:

'The value of a human life is infinite and beyond measure, so that any part of life – even if only an hour or a second – is of precisely the same worth as seventy years of it, just as any fraction of infinity, being indivisible, remains infinite.'[72]

Therefore, one who kills such a person, even if that person is in extreme pain and very near death, is still considered a murderer. Jewish law is explicit – both euthanasia and assisted suicide are prohibited. Indeed, even 'passive euthanasia' is sometimes prohibited when it involves the omission of certain therapeutic procedures or withholding medication, since physicians are charged with prolonging life.

However, teaching in the Talmud does advocate that there must be compassion for the suffering of a dying patient. And that whilst it is right to do everything to prolong life, Judaism does permit the death process

---

[71] See the Church and Society Council's report 2014, quoted at: https://churchofscotland.org.uk/about-us/our-views/end-of-life
[72] For more on the Orthodox Jewish view, see BBC Bitesize: https://www.bbc.co.uk/religion/religions/judaism/jewishethics/euthanasia.shtml

to occur with appropriate palliative care, if the patient wants that and their rabbi has ruled is acceptable.

NON-RELIGIOUS REPONSES

Right to Life UK
Right to Life UK is a charitable organisation focused on life issues including assisted suicide. They state that they are committed to an 'evidence-based approach to life issues', embracing a range of philosophical beliefs including non-religious, religious, and agnostic.

They argue that morally, there is no real difference between euthanasia and assisted suicide as both involve the intentional killing of human life. They believe that anyone requesting help to die is actually suffering from psychological distress, and requires psychological care rather than lethal drugs.

Further to this, they argue that any country that has legalised assisted dying has also made a statement about the value of its citizens' lives - effectively saying that some lives are more valuable, or more worthy of living, than others. To support this point, they ask people to consider how society usually responses when someone is suicidal: contending that we would originally seek to help dissuade them from doing so. However, for people who are disabled, very ill, frail, or close to death, the reaction for many people is quite different. They believe that to legal suicide for some, is effectively discriminatory, and if death is viewed as something to be avoided then that should be universally applied.

Spokesperson Dr Miro Griffiths argued, '*The development of Canada's euthanasia framework since it was introduced should trouble every politician in the UK who is being asked to back legal assisted suicide... cases of coercion and abuse, and worsening discrimination against marginalised groups are also part of the global picture. People feel forced to opt for assisted death because of poverty, homelessness, or a lack of care. These laws offer only an illusion of choice.*'[73]

---

[73] 'Assisted suicide plans in Scotland "regressive and dangerous" campaigners warn, *Right to Life News*, 29 December 2022:

Humanists

Whilst there is no one set Humanist position on any ethical issue, they will typically support a position that upholds values such as empathy, compassion, and respect for individual autonomy. Therefore unsurprisingly, many humanists support assisted dying for those who are suffering – if that is what they want.

They do not believe life has value purely by virtue of DNA or because of anything outwith ourselves, but rather it is up to each individual to decide whether their life is worth living; they believe that it's not enough to just be alive, but one needs to have conscious experiences – which include hopes and aspirations for the future. It follows that if a person is seeking help to relieve suffering, you ought to do so on the basis that this shows empathy for how they feel and also respects their freedom of thought. As American philosopher James Rachels wrote:

'From the point of view of the living individual, there is nothing important about being alive except that it enables one to have a life. In the absence of a conscious life, it is of no consequence to the subject himself whether he lives or dies… the mere persistence of your body has no importance.'

'Humanists UK' have considered several moral issues but believe that these concerns can be alleviated by proper safeguards. They make the point that by legalising assisted dying, it can be properly legislated to ensure that the vulnerable are not targeted. For example, counselling could be mandatory, checks could be put in place to ensure the patient is of sound mind and judgment, any instructions would need to be clearly witnessed and more than one doctor would need to approve of the care plan. They believe that by tightly defining these rules, a 'slippery slope' could be prevented. Further to this, they assert that it would also alleviate the need for people from the UK to travel to Switzerland for an assisted death. At present, this option is only available for those who can afford to do so, and for those who are able to travel. This may mean that people are seeking death earlier than they

---

https://righttolife.org.uk/news/assisted-suicide-plans-in-scotland-regressive-and-dangerous-campaigners-warn

would've ideally wanted and obviously, is not an option that is available to everyone.[74]

Kevin Yuill

American liberal humanist philosopher Kevin Yuill is strongly against assisted dying and euthanasia. He states that assisted dying does not promote autonomy because it approves of death for some (such as the terminally ill) but not others. He says *'it is not possible to say that individuals may freely choose death if we state that they may only do so in these certain situations'.*[75] Instead, he says assisted dying is devaluing the lives of those with terminal illness or chronic conditions and failing to respect them in the same way we would respect others who requested suicide: by trying to show them that we cared about them and they didn't need to end things. Also, by trying to enlist the help of others in the death, he says that assisted dying infringes on other people's autonomy. He also argues that assisted dying fails to be compassionate as it encourages people to see themselves as a burden on society. In this sense, ending a person's 'biographical' life is a real problem.

Yuill also notes that many thinkers in Britain want to legalise assisted suicide but stop short of wanting to legalise euthanasia. He says that they are morally equivalent and that if we are going to admit assisted dying it would be morally cowardly not to allow euthanasia too. In addition, he states that if someone is already in a vegetative state or has lost the ability to experience or communicate, the situation could be different. In these cases, he admits that the definition of death can seem to be blurred and there are some cases when withdrawing treatment is the kindest option.[76]

---

[74] See Humanists UK website for a more detailed explanation of their view on assisted dying: https://humanists.uk/campaigns/public-ethical-issues/assisted-dying/

[75] Kevin Yuill, *Assisted Suicide: The Liberal, Humanist Case against Legalization*, (Palgrave Macmillan, 2013), 57.

[76] Yuill, *Assisted Suicide*, 48.

DISCUSSION TASK: WHO CAN MAKE THE CHOICE?

All five of these people could request assisted suicide. In Scotland or elsewhere in Britain, this request would not currently be granted.

 Andre has a terminal cancer diagnosis and has six months to live.

 Boris was injured in a rugby accident and is paralysed from the waist down.

 Vanessa has dementia and is losing the ability to recognise her family.

 Micah has severe depression.

 Rhea is a Philosophy student and wants the ultimate adventure.

a) If the new assisted dying bill was passed in Scotland, who out of these people would be allowed assisted suicide?
b) In other countries such as Switzerland and the Netherlands, who would be allowed assisted suicide? (research the specific laws in different countries if you want)
c) Who would a member of the Church of Scotland think should be allowed assisted suicide?
d) Who would Humanists think should be allowed assisted suicide? What other questions might they ask to try to ensure vulnerable people were safeguarded?
e) Kevin Yuill and other opponents of assisted suicide argue that to allow it to some but not all of these people is to assign different values to human lives and does not promote autonomy. Are they right?
f) What could be the moral implications of allowing assisted suicide for Rhea?
g) Who (if anyone) would you allow to access assisted suicide? Why?

h) Would any of your earlier answers be different if you were discussing euthanasia instead of assisted suicide? How and why?

ABOUT THE AUTHORS

Laura Crichton is a teacher of Religious, Moral, and Philosophical Studies at Stewart's Melville College, Edinburgh. She gained her MA in Divinity at the University of Aberdeen, before completing her PGDE at the University of Edinburgh. She has taught Advanced Higher RMPS since 2009 and is a marker for the Scottish Qualifications Authority - at both Higher and Advanced Higher. Before teaching, she served in the Royal Signals Corps and now is the Contingent Commander of the schools' CCF. She enjoys teaching immensely provided she has a cup of coffee in hand.

Dr Susan Woodshore teaches at the Mary Erskine School in Edinburgh. She has an MA in English from Cambridge University, MTh and PhD in historical theology from the University of Edinburgh and a PGCE from the University of East Anglia. Before teaching, she worked as a freelance editor and copywriter. She has been teaching since 2015, including Advanced Higher Medical Ethics since 2017. She enjoys encouraging students to be open-minded and question everything, but if you want to distract her from teaching just ask her about the parrot.

Printed in Great Britain
by Amazon

31216596R10076